West Virginia Railroads
Volume 4: Virginian Railway

Lloyd D. Lewis

Quarrier press

Charleston, West Virginia

I dedicate this new book to my son Carter David Glenn Lewis and his new bride Amber – and also to my nephew Glenn Parker Lewis, who has followed in his Uncle Lloyd's footsteps by teaching English overseas. Hope you just loved both South Korea and Nepal, young man!

My Love and Very Best Wishes to You.....Now and Always!

This dedication also certainly extends to all Virginian Railway employees who ever drew a paycheck from The Virginian, Deepwater and Tidewater Railways. I sincerely wish that I could have been counted among ye.

Lloyd D. Lewis

Kenova, West Virginia
November 1st, 2011.

Digital Photo Production, Design, and Layout by Karen Parker

Digital Reformatting by Mark S. Phillips

Distributed by:

West Virginia Book Company
1125 Central Avenue
Charleston, West Virginia 25302
www.wvbookco.com

Front Cover: EL-2B No. 128, flying the while flags on an extra, heads eastward over the big curving trestle above the town of Covel in this 1949 photo. The train consists entirely of Virginian's hulking 100+ ton gondolas that could only be unloaded by rotary dumpers, and therefore were heavily used in the coalfields-to-Sewalls Point Piers service. (George King Shands Photo, Lloyd D. Lewis collection, colorized by Karen Parker)

Title Page: Covel, West Virginia, with its long curving trestle was always a favorite of Virginian photographers, and here class EL-3A No. 107 has an extra east of 28 loads at 10:23 a.m., June 14, 1950. (Richard J. Cook Photo, TLC collection)

Facing Page: EL-2B No. 128 is westbound with a train of empty hoppers, returning them to the mines to be filled yet again. This nice photo was taken at the Clarks Gap substation, probably in the summer of 1948. (Ben F. Cutler photo, Lloyd D. Lewis collection)

Back Cover Top Left: VGN DE-RS Train Master as East End Elmore Yard switcher on the eastbound double track mainline passing what is probably a two-unit EL-C rectifier electric returning light from pushing a Hill Run to Clarks Gap. "END of CTC TERRITORY" sign applies to lead track that runs behind the former Elmore Steam Shop out of sight to right that was non-signaled in those days. Date is 1959. (Gene Huddleston photo, Lloyd D. Lewis collection)

Back Cover Top Right: Train Time at Oak Hill Junction – October, 1954. Extra 718 East with class USA 2-8-8-2 No. 718 and class USE 2-8-8-2 No. 736 and a trainload of coal from the mines around Page thunders up the 2.02% grade past Oak Hill Junction. Highballing the eastbound is W. G. Lewis, the author's father, who was the VGN's last Supervisor of Telegraph and Signals. He's been out here with signal maintainer Earl May since before dawn clearing up signal trouble so as to not delay this train. (This painting by Andrew Harmantas was done for and appeared on the cover of the author's earlier book The Virginian Era, also published by TLC in 1992)

Back Cover Bottom: Eastbound loads behind EL-3A No. 100 pass east end of Princeton Yard with the depot buildings and Princeton Shops in left far background. Mid-1950s. (Jeffry L. Sanders collection)

Table of Contents

Foreword

This is the fourth in our series of books that details the major railroads that operated in the state of West Virginia. The book *West Virginia Railroads - Railroading in the Mountain State*, published in 2009, is an overview and introduction to the railroads that operated in West Virginia, with a short historic, photographic, and map treatment of each. Follow-on books such as this build from that basic overview with more photos, maps, and details.

The treatment of the Virginian Railway in the past has been fairly sparse. H. Reid's *Virginian Railway* (Kalmbach Publishing, 1961) was the first full-length book about the line. The only other books that have treated the Virginian, its history and equipment in any detail are *Virginian Railway Handbook* (by Aubrey Wiley and Conley Wallace, W-W Publishing, 1985), *The Virginian Era* (Lewis, TLC Publishing, 1992), *Virginian Railway Locomotives* (Lewis, TLC Publishing, 1993), *Norfolk & Western and Virginian Railway in Color* (H. Reid, edited by Lewis, TLC Publishing, 1994), *Virginian Rails* (Kurt Reisweber, Old Line Graphics, 1995), *Virginian Railway in Color* (William G. McClure III and Jeremy F. Plant, Morning Sun Books, 2005), and *Virginian Railway Pictorial* (Aubrey Wiley, 2010). Aside from that, some small equipment photo books have been published by Bob's Photos, and there have been numerous articles and other data about the Virginian published by the N&W Historical Society and other magazines. Most recently, in 2010 Aubrey Wiley published his hardbound volume *Virginian Railway Pictorial*.

Volume 1 of the TLC West Virginia series devoted only 16 pages to the Virginian. We now seek to expand that coverage in the present volume with more photos as well as maps, drawings, plats, and additional historical background on equipment. It is hoped that it can serve as a good reference work for the Virginian as it operated within the borders of the state of West Virginia. With the maps, as well as yard and track diagrams, we hope it will be more of a "gazetteer," to which the reader may refer. It is also hoped that it will be a readable book that will explain how the Virginian operated in West Virginia, especially in the era from World War II to the early diesel era, a period in which there is much interest.

The bulk of the photos are in the 1930-1965 era. This was a time of transition, when the railways stopped being the dominant intercity carriers, yielding ever more to highway and air travel and competition from barges on navigable rivers. It was also the era when steam locomotives reached the pinnacle of their development and then suddenly were wiped away by diesel-electric technology. It was the time when passenger trains, and all that they meant to ordinary people, reached a high state of efficiency and then quickly declined. Concomitant with these changes were the elimination and consolidation of stations, yards, and facilities; the abandonment of no longer profitable branches; and the shift of railroads from common carriage to bulk-materials transport. This was especially so in West Virginia, where coal was (and is) the major commodity that railroads transported.

Unlike the other railroads of West Virginia, which were all parts of larger systems covering many states and carrying diverse products in addition to their large coal traffic, the Virginian was almost exclusively involved in coal traffic from West Virginia across Virginia to the port at Norfolk. But it did have some merchandise freight service and it had local passenger trains that served its mainline and some coal branches.

The passenger service consisted of local-style accommodation coach-only trains that served the people who lived along its line, an obligatory requirement in the era before alternate transportation was available.

Virginian was famous for its electrified operations and for the great "Streamliner" electrics that were the ultimate expression of that technology. In steam locomotives, Virginian opted for unparalleled power, and rostered some of the most powerful steam of all time.

Built very late in the railway age, it benefited from modern engineering and was a highly developed line in its physical plant.

Always a money-maker, the Virginian ultimately became part of the Norfolk & Western's system in 1959. It is widely remembered today and of great interest to railfans and modelers.

Lloyd Lewis, a life-long Virginian historian, has compiled this material from his large collection and knowledge of the line.

Thomas W. Dixon, Jr.
TLC Publishing
September, 2011

The Virginian Railway was one of the world's shortest Class I category railway companies, yet it hauled millions of tons of southern West Virginia Pocahontas seam soft bituminous coal, also known as "smokeless coal."

Planned and constructed using more than $40 million of his quite substantial funds by one very wealthy man – Henry Huddleston Rogers – the 611-mile-long railroad originally started at the Kanawha River's south shore at a whistle stop named Deepwater on the Chesapeake & Ohio Railway, about 35 miles southeast of Charleston, the capital of West Virginia.

The way Rogers thought out his line was to use the absolute best technology available at the beginning of the Twentieth Century, which was just about as good as it still is a hundred years later.

His managers, engineers and laborers spared no expense whatsoever and kept bridges, grade and tunnels to a minimum and yet traversed the landscape – particularly in the four counties traversed in West Virginia – in the shortest distance possible.

Colonel William Nelson Page, a civil engineer and railroad planner who lived in a lovely mansion in Ansted, Fayette County, befriended Rogers about 1895 and together they pursued the latter's dream of getting the coal from his New York City partners' spectacular deposits eventually to the sea. Rogers' mining partners included Abraham Hewitt, a former mayor of New York City.

Rogers, a native of Fairhaven, Massachusetts, and his partner William Morrison Flagler were early close associates of John D. Rockefeller in the original Standard Oil Company and made millions for their efforts. Flagler used his money to build the Florida East Coast Railroad from Jacksonville to Miami and then to Key West, Florida. VGN's goal was to transport coal by the most efficient railway possible to one – and later two – piers at Sewalls Point near Norfolk, Virginia, measured at 435 miles from the C&O at Deepwater Station.

Rogers' first step was to buy the four-mile-long Loup Creek & Deepwater Railway, soon reorganized and shortened to just Deepwater, a logging road from a sawmill at Robson, down the steep grades of Loup Creek to the C&O, boring through Big Right Hand and Big Left Hand tunnels on the way.

Then his idea was to sell out to either or both the C&O and Norfolk & Western Railways – and start another similar project. He had accomplished this twice and perhaps three times before in West Virginia and this proved to be a good scheme to confuse the larger railroad in each case by forcing it to buy his little line or face extraordinary competition. He learned these tricks early at Standard Oil, earning the nickname "Hell Hound Rogers." But this time, one of the world's best kept business secrets and scurrilous skullduggery became necessary when he, using Colonel Page as his exclusive "front man" in the big city negotiations, could not reach satisfactory – to Rogers, that is – coal rates with the C&O at Deepwater or the N&W at a little Mercer County town named Matoaka.

No one was going to outdo Rogers and his millions – and he soon proved it. So from his New York City office, he sent Colonel Page and several crews to work surveying a spectacular railway named the Tidewater several hundred miles to the East Coast.

This is the extreme extents in which they operated: One Sunday in February 1904, several three-man survey crews equipped with fishing poles as well as transits detrained at several points from an eastbound N&W daytime local passenger train which ran from Bluefield, West Virginia, along the south bank of New River to Roanoke, Virginia.

One wonders what the train crew thought of so many "fishermen" wading the shallow depths of New River – one of the world's oldest, by the way – on a winter Sunday. No matter what they thought, for by day's end, the surveyors had boarded other N&W local or mixed trains, finished their surveys and maps, paid the small fees and filed them the next day or so in courthouses in Pearisburg, Giles County, Christiansburg, Montgomery County, and Salem, Roanoke County, Virginia. The deed was partially done.

Thus, the plot of this mystery thickens–and no one except Colonel Page knew who was paying for all this work. And neither N&W nor C&O knew the better for quite a long time!

In the meantime, Rogers' lawyers carried out their boss's orders and merged the Deepwater and Tidewater Railways into The Virginian Railway Company, incorporating the latter on March 8, 1907, in Richmond, Virginia.

Flash forward to April 26, 1909, the day and time set for Rogers to officially drive home the probable last iron spike into the wooden tie at the west end of his new Virginian Railway's longest and about its most spectacular bridge, the half-mile-long span over New River just east of the Virginia – West Virginia state line at the village of Glen Lyn, Virginia.

Rogers's best friend, the world-famous Mark Twain, was not on this first and best-known official inspection train ever to traverse the entire VGN. Twain had taken his wealthy associate's yacht "Kanawha" back to New York City because he did not like to ride trains.

The westbound train chugged on past Glen Lyn and over the West Virginia mountains for two more days, staying overnight in both Princeton and then Bud on the west slope of Clarks Gap Mountain on this, the world's newest railroad. The first night on this new and still settling-down roadbed was in Roanoke.

This memorable trip was the only time Rogers got to see his $40 million-plus investment because he died at home in New York City the next month, May 1909.

From that time until Virginian was bought out by N&W on December 1st, 1959, "The Richest Little Railway in the World" lived up to its name – and then some! Spectacularly profitable because of its great quantities of on-line rich veins of soft coal and also because it was not burdened with much passenger service, VGN made money literally "hand over fist" in nearly every one of its 52 years of existence.

In fact, the longer the line was listed on the New York Stock Exchange, the more profitable it became. In the late 1950s its operating ratio – the percentage of revenue the railway spent on its operations each year – was in the absolutely unheard of mid-40s.

In other words, for each dollar VGN took in, the company's profit was more than 50 cents. No wonder N&W and C&O both tried to take over VGN in the 1920s and then N&W finally grabbed up VGN on its probably charmed third attempt.

This outstanding railway always had the best of managers – literally the best that money could buy! These men were always free to innovate and experiment with the sizes and power of their locomotives, cars and their capacities and the methods of operation.

From the company's Mechanical Department headquarters in the small, 10,000-population Mercer County seat of Princeton, West Virginia, men like George Byron Halstead, Superintendents of Motive Power and engineers like the Slayton Brothers, originally of Michigan, John William Sasser, J. W. Kirkhu and the final one, W. W. Osborne, set the car and locomotive policies.

These talented men and their small staffs designed these railroad monsters and spent the big bucks.

The money, of course, to implement the Princeton men's well-planned and always innovative concoctions came from the company's president and board of directors at headquarters in Norfolk Terminal Station.

However, one of the most successful in operation besides dieselization in the early and mid 1950s resulted from a nasty, prolonged strike that shut down the entire railroad in 1923. Steam locomotive crews nearly died of asphyxiation and suffocation due to hellish conditions they had to endure day after day and year after year on the two-percent-plus Clarks Gap Mountain grade.

What these men had to put up with is nearly unimaginable in the present day. This "Hell On Wheels" started in the first tunnel east of Garwood, Wyoming County, as the men scurried to jump into water tanks, used wet cotton waste to cover their faces and hooked up their emergency hoods and rubber hoses in a desperate attempt to find fresh air just to stay alive!

Head end brakeman even affixed wooden chairs to the front pilots of their huge locomotives to get through the several long tunnels ahead of the smoke belching stacks. Micajah Tunnel itself was nearly a mile long.

If that were not bad enough, crews on the generally two end-of-train pushers had it even worse because of putrid smoke still lingering in the long bore. But even that wasn't as bad as those men who really suffered in wooden cabooses on the rear.

The nearly unbelievable conditions did not end until the very sturdy head end crewmen's long heavy coal drags burst with a gigantic "WHOOSH!" of black steam and smoke through the east postal of Clarks Gap Tunnel at Algonquin coal camp. And this all occurred for about 15 years, getting worse with each change of new and improved steam locomotives which put out more and more smoke and steam!

What exact event provoked the long strike of 1922-3 against the VGN is probably lost to history. However, the labor action certainly did occur and train crews got other jobs, some getting new train and engine service positions on the Florida East Coast Railroad.

This author met a union representative with the Brotherhood of Locomotive Engineers in my home town of Princeton in the 1970s. His local's dwindling membership still considered themselves to be on strike against The Virginian Railway Company – 50-plus years hence!

Unless this strike had not shut down this railway at this time, the massive improvement in operating efficiency would not have happened at the time. Thus, Virginian may never have electrified its 136-mile-long mainline from Mullens, West Virginia, to Roanoke Virginia, completing this huge task in September 1926.

The writer recently found an advertisement for VGN's large three-unit Westinghouse electric engines, of which the line owned 36 units. Of all the statistics proving how VGN was so profitable and made more money per mile of track than ANY in the world and how its operating ratio was absolutely the lowest for decades quoted therein, one really stands out.

Following the damaging and morale-killing engineman's strike, electrification enabled VGN to cut its system wide operating costs by an astounding forty-five percent. And that only involved the most mountainous subdivision, which is about 25 percent of the entire property. This is truly an amazing statistic in comparison with other railroads.

The Great Depression of the 1930s really debilitated the economy of the entire world, but VGN was not as hard hit as most companies, or railroads in particular. VGN never went bankrupt, for one thing, and even continued to pay small dividends all during this terrible period in our history.

The company's efficiencies and fabulous economic base served it well throughout its entire corporate life. VGN even had the largest coal-carrying gondola cars. The rich little line definitely ran the longest and heaviest trains in the world on a regular basis. And all on a 600-mile-long railroad.

From 1909 through the huge steamers, electrics and diesel-electrics, VGN consistently owned and its crews operated the world's most powerful and most spectacular locomotives – and was willing to try anything to keep its trains moving better all the time.

Both C&O and N&W employed Lima Locomotive Works' most interesting products, Shay geared steam locomotives, to go against their roughest grades on both mainline and coal branches. Usually used on primitive trackage on remote, crudely built logging lines, Shays will pull or push just about anything – but only at a top speed of about 10 m.p.h.

C&O owned about 12 giant four-truck Shays and used them on branches in West Virginia's New River Gorge. N&W put into service a single four-trucker on its mainline pushing coal drags eastbound up Bluefield Mountain from around Iaeger about 45 miles up to Bluefield, West Virginia.

Quite lopsided and anything but handsome, these tough beasts of burden satisfied managements of both roads for only a few years until bigger and better steam monsters entered the fray.

This writer has a typewritten note of history written by the above mentioned George Byron Halstead in which he states that VGN certainly considered Shays for Clarks Gap Mountain. But instead VGN went with a massive but very underpowered Triplex experiment with a wheel arrangement of 2-8-8-8-4, 10 huge 2-10-10-2s – which the author maintains are the most underappreciated locomotives VGN ever rostered – and eventually 52 units of record-busting electrics and 25 mighty 2,400-horsepower diesel-electrics.

This was VGN at its best – always building the biggest and most powerful of anything ever assembled up to that date.

And most astounding are VGN's steam diagrams that mechanical artists had in their fertile minds for proposed but never built giants of the rails. They even envisioned locos with wheel arrangements as imaginative and wild as featuring 40 driving wheels.

Even though VGN never considered hiring a corporate public relations staff – of even one person – its spectacular earnings and operating world records – year after year – made rail industry headlines in both trade journals and the popular press.

One long article in the April 1939 issue of *Railroad Magazine* ballyhooed the company as a "Transportation Factory," which it surely was. And those smart moves from years before served N&W very well and still are helping Norfolk Southern today.

Dieselization with all Fairbanks-Morse large units – except for little No. 6, a 44-ton General Electric switcher for Suffolk, Virginia's, Planter's Peanuts plants – came later than most other formerly all-steam lines. Last run for VGN steam was on the evening of June 1, 1957, as ex-C&O 0-8-0 No. 251 ran only half its second trick on Princeton Yard before being replaced with a brand-new 1,600-horsepower F-M unit

Fairbanks-Morse "Train Masters" of 2,400 horse-power were really in control as proven by the railway's 1954 annual report, which featured on both front and back covers prints made from 4x5 Ektachrome film taken by Narrows (Virginia) Power Plant General Foreman George King Shands, who doubled as the company's official photographer.

Shands and his VGN colleague Mr. Burgess from Norfolk, had Princeton West End Dispatcher Arthur Perry stop Time Freight No 72 atop the then clear view available from Slab Fork Bridge about 10 miles west of Mullens for some memorable shots on a beautiful day probably in the fall of 1953.

The personal meaning for this author in the front cover photo was my Dad's 1954 light blue Ford sedan in the right background parked against the standard wooden Slab Fork Station. His Signal Supervisor duties had taken him that day to this coal camp and he had already spoken to depot agent Bernice ("Si") Coleman, who in the 1920s had his own travelling hillbilly band and who also had written a train song titled "The Wreck of the C&O Number 5."

"Little Slick" Inge, a VGN West End Trainmaster, whose brother Aubrey ("Big Slick") Inge, was company claim agent in Princeton at that time, is shown leaning out of the brand Train Master's fireman's side window in both shots.

There followed in 1956-57 12 new ignitron rectifier electric engines from General Electric. After the four new million-pounder 1948 "Streamliner" electrics, also from GE, this dozen units were VGN's third and last class of electric locomotive, and futuristic railroad expert John W. Barrier termed the "rectifiers" just about the brightest development in rail motive power in many a year.

Virginian's final act was its corporate disillusionment and merger into arch competitor N&W on the above mentioned December 1st, 1959, followed closely by scrapping all its remaining steam power

in January, 1960, except SA Class 0-8-0 No. 4, whic is now in the Virginia Museum of Transportation i Roanoke.

Also gone after about 8 p.m. Saturday of June 3 1962, was VGN's by then 35-year old electrificatio as Power Director Charles C. Linkenhoker shut dow the final coal-powered turbine in the Narrows Pow Plant on the north bank of New River.

Between that time and now much of the railway mainline line east of Roanoke is gone, as is most the double-track mainline over Clarks Gap Moun tain, as well as other small abandonments – plus th relocation of about 20 miles of the Guyan River Lin because of the R. D. Bailey Dam.

It was a mighty fascinating run for just mo than 52 years. The Virginian concept all began the mind of the memorable and very wealthy Hen Huddleston Rogers about 1896. Never has there ev been a better example of the famous old adage that corporation "is the extension of one man's shadow."

With its two VGN predecessors, the Deepwat and the Tidewater, built toward each other in secr – at least from competitors N&W and C&O – startin in 1904, and they were joined at the west end of th majestic 2,155-foot-long New River Bridge at Gle Lyn, Virginia, in January 1909.

For several recent years, the Norfolk Souther honored VGN as it did none of its other predecess roads. VGN, the NS website noted, had a very loy group of employees, many of which worked for th railroad during its entire existence. Such a fine tri ute!

As first Virginian Railway book author H. Re quoted Miss Laura Kincaid of Kincaid, West Virgini at the textual end of his tome, "There will always a Virginian." Amen to that.

The Mainline

The Virginian mainline westward out of Roanoke, Virginia, entered West Virginia as crossed New River near the town of Glen Lyn, Virginia. Westward from that point it passed through the towns of Kellysville, Oakvale, Stengel and Ingleside before arriving at Princeton. It was at Princeton that VGN established its main shop and mechanical headquarters. A large two-story station was erected here, as well as an extensive shop complex, which was capable of repairing the large steam locomotives that the line rostered over the years. The shop also took care of the railway's freight and passenger car fleet. Princeton became very much a railroad town, with the VGN as its major employer in the high days of steam operations.

Although the VGN line climbed in elevation almost continuously after leaving the near sea-level Sewalls Point at Norfolk, from Roanoke west it had the steepest rise, climbing the Blue Ridge to a summit at Merrimac, Va., then down along the New River until crossing the West Virginia border. From there to Princeton the rise was 1.35% for about ten miles. At Princeton the line dipped once again and then climbed to Clark's Gap, where the famous Clarks Gap Tunnel carried it under the ridge line. West of there the line was on a very steep grade, as much as 2.07% downward, westbound; but, of course, upgrade for the important traffic of the VGN: eastbound coal. Located at the base of the Clarks Gap grade was Mullens and the nearby Elmore yard, which served as the main marshalling yard for Virginian's coal fields branches. These are treated later in this book.

It was the Clarks Gap portion of the main line, mentioned elsewhere in this book, that was the ruling grade for VGN's heavy coal trains, and it was this service that was the driving element in the company's development of its massive steam locomotives. This was also the region over which the Virginian installed its famous electrified operations, covered in detail in other parts of this book, stretching between Mullens

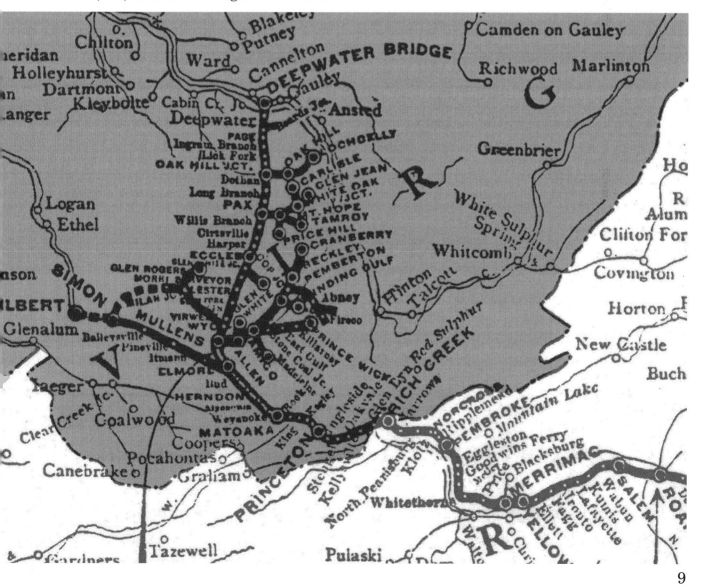

across the West Virginia portions of its mainline and on into Roanoke.

The portion of the mainline between the state line and Matoaka had little coal production, and other traffic was sparse in the rural and largely isolated region. Mines along the mainline between Princeton and Mullens included Covel, Herndon, Tierney, Gaston, Deerfield, and Tralee. Other Virginian-served mines lay on the main line and many branch lines to the west of Mullens.

The line from Roanoke to Elmore was known on the Virginian as the Third Sub-Division. Beyond Elmore lay the Fourth Sub-Division, running generally geographically north to Deepwater on the Kanawha River. Leaving Mullens, the line followed Slab Fork through the towns of Maben, Hotchkiss, and Slab Fork. At Slab Fork, the line climbed out of the valley of Slab Fork Creek, crossing above the creek and town on a massive steel trestle, and passing through a short tunnel at Jenny Gap.

From there the road followed the Skinner Fork and Surveyor Creek through Lester and Surveyor to

Glen White, where it turned up Piney Creek to E‑ cles, and then up the Millers Camp Branch to Harpe From Harper it was downhill again along the uppe reaches of Paint Creek through Sweenyburg to Pa site of the interchange with shortline Kanawha, Gle Jean, and Eastern, and thence to Lively.

Beyond Lively the road left Paint Creek, crosse the ridge through a short tunnel, and entered th Mossy Creek watershed. Following Mossy Cree the line came to Oak Hill Junction, where the Whit Oak Branch joined the main line. Oak Hill Junctio was also where the line started following Loop Cree down toward the Kanawha River, passing throug Page along the way. Page was the site of the majo yard and engine terminal on the west end of the rai road. From Page the railroad followed Loop Cree westward (geographic northward) and down to th Kanawha River, where the junction with the Che apeake and Ohio was located at Deepwater, on th south side of the river. The VGN then crossed th river to DB Tower, on the north side, and a junctio with the New York Central's Kanawha and Michiga Line after 1931.

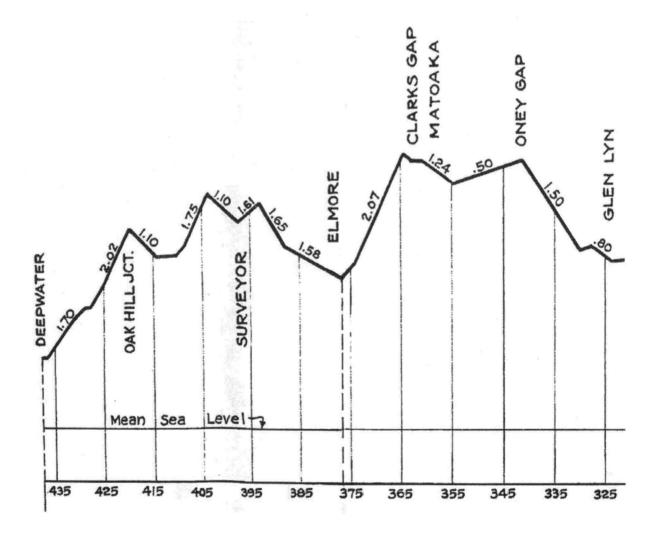

10

Station Number	Miles from Norfolk	Third Sub-Division STATIONS
324	323.8	GLEN LYN
		2.0
326	325.8	HALES GAP
		2.0
328	327.8	KELLYSVILLE
		2.0
330	329.8	OAKVALE
		5.4
335	335.2	INGLESIDE
		5.0
340	340.2	PRINCETON
		4.8
345	345.0	KEGLEY
		3.6
349	348.6	KING
		2.9
352	351.5	ROCK
		4.0
355	355.5	M. X. TOWER
		0.7
356	356.2	MATOAKA
		1.5
358	357.7	WEYANOKE
		3.1
360	360.8	CLARKS GAP
		0.5
361	361.3	ALGONQUIN
		2.0
364	363.3	MICAJAH
		3.1
366	366.4	COVEL
		1.4
368	367.8	HERNDON
		3.3
371	371.1	BUD
		0.9
372	372.0	ALPOCA
		1.9
374	373.9	TRALEE
		0.8
375	374.7	ELMORE

(DOUBLE TRACK noted vertically alongside rows 355–368)

Station Number	Miles from Norfolk	Fourth Sub-Division STATIONS
375	374.7	ELMORE
		1.8
	376.5	GULF JUNCTION
		0.2
377	376.7	MULLENS
		1.4
378	378.1	HARMCO
		1.2
379	379.3	OTSEGO
		1.1
381	380.4	VIRWEST
		1.3
382	381.7	MABEN
		3.9
386	385.6	HOTCHKISS
		2.3
388	387.9	SLAB FORK
		2.2
390	390.1	JENNY GAP
		2.1
392	392.2	LESTER
		2.5
395	394.7	SURVEYOR
		1.6
396	396.3	GLEN WHITE JUNCTION
		0.6
397	396.9	SEMOCO
		1.7
399	398.6	ECCLES
		2.0
401	400.6	HARPER
		3.5
404	404.1	SWEENEYBURG
		2.3
406	406.4	CIRTSVILLE
		1.6
408	408.0	WILLIS BRANCH
		1.1
409	409.1	PAX
		0.8
410	409.9	LONG BRANCH
		1.7
412	411.6	LIVELY
		3.2
415	414.8	DOTHAN
		2.0
417	416.8	SILVER GAP
		0.9
418	417.7	OAK HILL JUNCTION
		2.2
420	419.9	LICK FORK
		1.2
421	421.1	WRISTON
		1.8
423	422.9	INGRAM BRANCH
		0.5
424	423.4	HAMILTON
		3.4
427	426.8	PAGE
		3.5
430	430.3	BEARDS FORK JUNCTION
		0.5
431	430.8	ROBSON
		3.3
434	434.1	VACO JUNCTION
		0.5
	434.6	WEST DEEPWATER
		0.4
435	435	D. B. TOWER
	466.5	CHARLESTON N. Y. C.

(CENTRALIZED TRAFFIC CONTROL TERRITORY noted vertically alongside the Fourth Sub-Division rows)

Opposite: Profile of the VGN main line in West Virginia, from Glen Lyn at the east to Deepwater at the west. (C&O Historical Society collection)

Above and Right: Station lists for the VGN main line in West Virginia. The Third Sub-Division ran from Roanoke, Va. to Elmore, W.Va., and the Fourth Sub-Division ran from Elmore to Deepwater W.Va. (Lloyd L. Lewis collection)

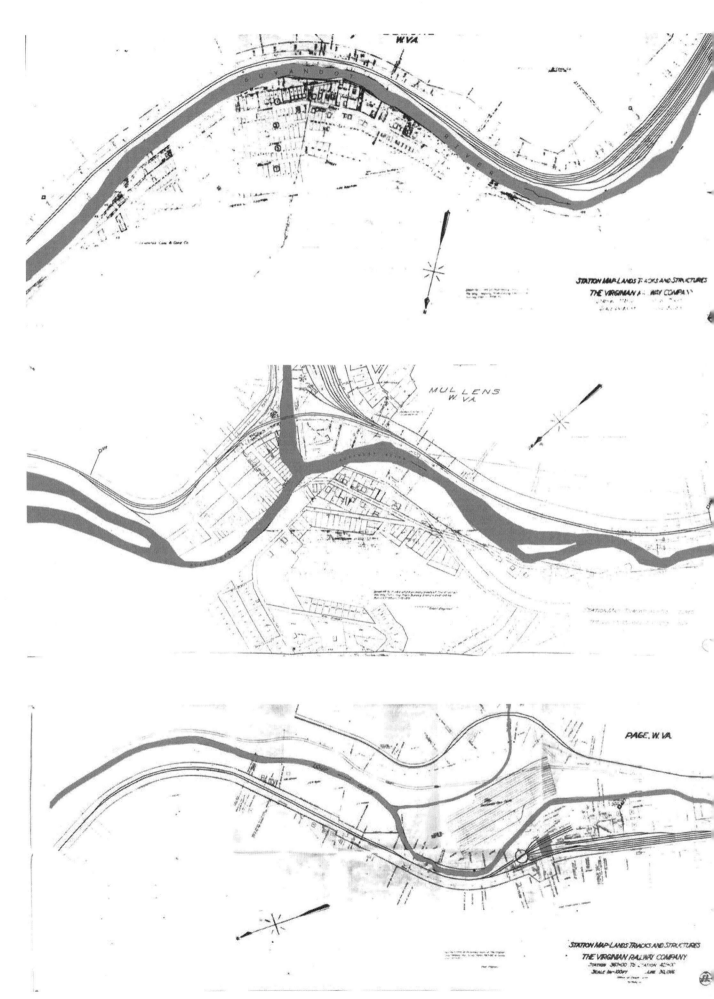

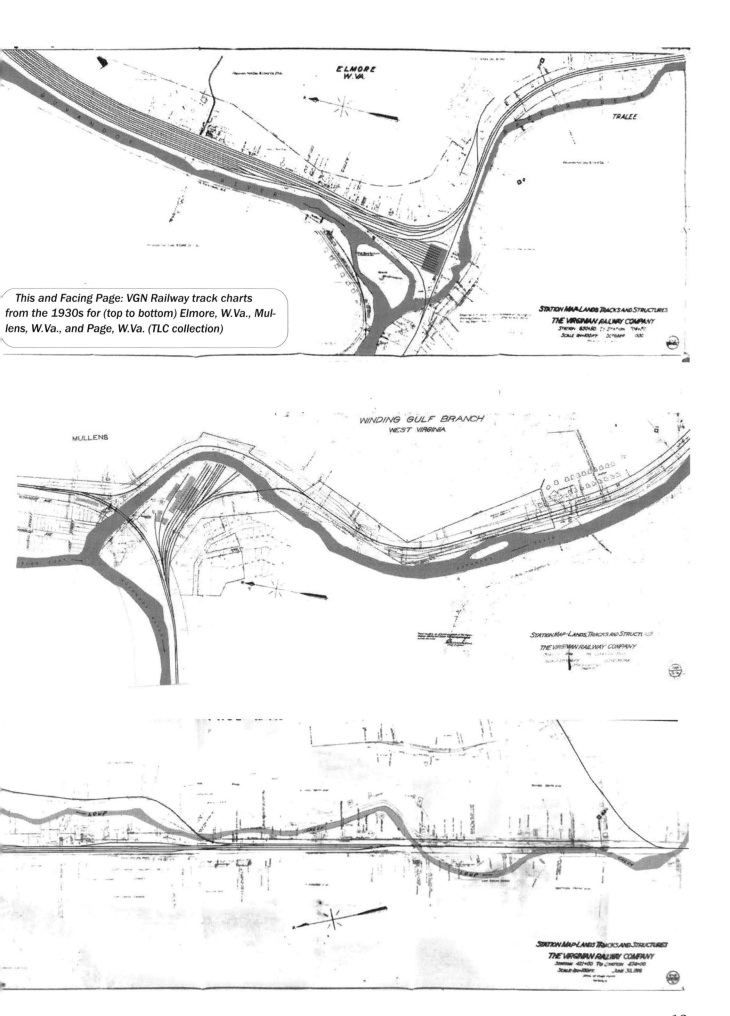

This and Facing Page: VGN Railway track charts from the 1930s for (top to bottom) Elmore, W.Va., Mullens, W.Va., and Page, W.Va. (TLC collection)

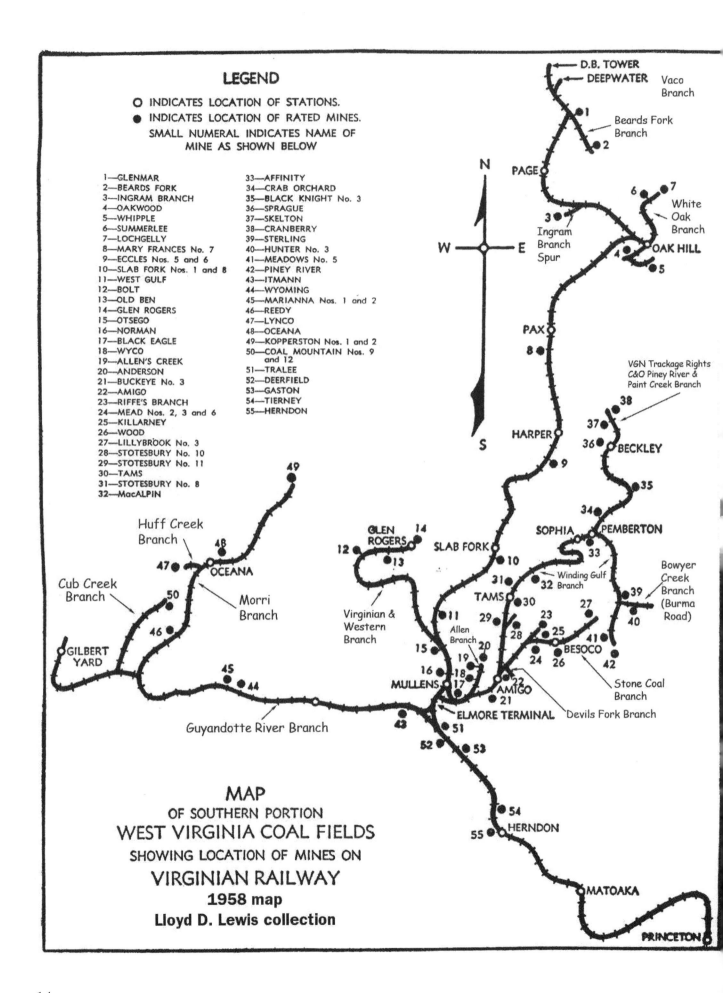

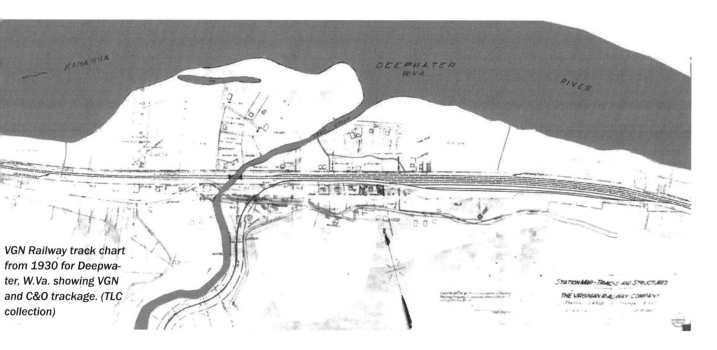

VGN Railway track chart from 1930 for Deepwater, W.Va. showing VGN and C&O trackage. (TLC collection)

Branch Lines

Guyandotte River Branch

The Virginian Railway Guyandotte River Branch is 44.4 miles long and was constructed in the mid-1930s from Elmore yard, immediately east of Mullens westbound through Jazbo, a former W. M. Ritter company lumber camp, through Pineville and a rich coalfield section to Gilbert Yard.

Gilbert was where this route ended and was where it connected with both the Norfolk & Western and Chesapeake & Ohio railways. Gilbert is also the only location where all three Pocahontas Roads connected with each other.

Building of this vital line was the result of a long legal battle between the three lines before the Interstate Commerce Commission for more than 10 years. In dealing with this subject, author J. T. Lambie in his scholarly and well-received *From Mine to Market* N&W history of 1954 titled this appropriate chapter "Making Terms With An Invader." N&W was getting pretty tired of having to put up with VGN by this time.

About 30 years before this line was laid out along the Guyandotte, W. M. Ritter Lumber Company began logging virgin timber about 1905 from Elmore Yard through "Paul Green" camp and the later established Itmann coal camp, named for coal operator Isaac T. Mann. We must note here that Ritter did not need ICC permission to build this line because of its non-common carrier status.

Westbound down the river to Pineville and over a wooden trestle across the Guyandotte at Castle Rock, Ritter placed his track on the back side of this village and logged as far west as near Oceana. Here another logging company, Cole & Crane, bought timber rights to do this on adjacent land.

Ritter connected with a narrow gauge line which built several miles up Pinnacle Creek Hollow toward the McDowell County line. Several years after the VGN-N&W merger, U.S. Steel dug a high-producing coal mine up this hollow and N&W served it with its Pinnacle Creek Spur. NS service continues to this day to another mine owner.

At least one other of Ritter's rough logging lines was built across the Guyandotte River west up into present-day Twin Falls State Park just east of Itmann. See Virginian & Western Branch story (page 21) for more on narrow-gauge Ritter activities building down from the north side of this wonderful state park.

A great friend of this author's from the Virginian days was the late Thomas J. Nichols, first a VGN train and engine service crewman and long a Trainmaster out of Elmore Yard and over the entire West End and New River Division. Tommy's father was Ritter's log train conductor for many years, which operated with a Shay six days per week from and to Maben sawmill to the end of Guyan River Line logging at Pineville from about 1905 until the mill closed about 1945.

Tommy's father was killed in this service. The 1905 Shay, built new for Maben Ritter service, was transferred several times to other mills and logging railroads and is now awaiting restoration at the Cass Scenic Railroad in Pocahontas County, West Virginia.

What this author would really like to see would be as many photos as possible of this Shay and its relatively tiny log train deep in Elmore yard seemingly squeezed between VGN giants like Class AE 2-10-10-2s, even larger EL-3A electrics and the huge 120 ton-capacity Class G-3 and Class G-4 gondolas.

Who can paint such an unforgettable scene as the daylight fades from this Deep West Virginia Hollow? – where the sun always came up at 10 a.m. and set at 2 p.m., as we used to say.

The original VGN Guyan River Line and its two branches – the Morri and Coal Mountain routes – were constructed too late to have hosted regular passenger train service. Decent driveable roads reached into the hills this far away from the state capital at Charleston by the mid-1930s.

Thus, other than office car inspection trains and track geometry trains, this route has had – to the best of this writer's knowledge – only two public excursions.

These runs were (1) the July 4, 1963, run from Elmore Yard to the original Cub Creek Junction and back sponsored by the Pineville Lions Club and (2) the July 4, 1975, eastbound only public fantrip sponsored by the Roanoke Chapter, National Railway Historical Society. This train was headed up by former Southern Railway 2-8-2 No. 4501 and N&W's newly repainted SD-45 No. 1776. It was one of the first revenue trips over this 20-mile-long new piece of railroad.

A one-time 1960 C&O office car special with two GP9s and a long train of C&O business cars made the journey from Raleigh yard south of Beckley, down both VGN's Winding Gulf and Guyandotte River branches from Elmore yard through Itmann – where this author saw this most unusual run – to Gilbert Yard and back onto C&O rails there.

This special probably was run in the summer of 1960 to confirm and explore C&O's trackage rights through this territory as a result of the ICC merger agreement between VGN and N&W effective the past December 1st.

So far as I know, this run has never been duplicated. However, the trackage rights agreements still exist into the 21st Century but have never been used on a regular basis on the Guyandotte River Branch portion. Also, these trackage rights are still shown on the CSX Transportation maps and have been on every map since 1960. The line from Gilbert Yard to Elmore Yard was used several times during the year in both steam and diesel-electric days for rerouting N&W passenger trains when derailments occurred blocking the larger road's double-track Pocahontas Division mainline.

Memorable photos were taken in the early 1950 by a trio of railfans who were thankfully there at tha right time as VGN Mikado No. 468 stormed upgrad from Elmore Yard to Clarks Gap in front of a shinin N&W J Class 4-8-4. The 2-8-2 was added after th J had brought N&W Train 4, *The Pocahontas*, over from Wharncliffe on the N&W main and up the sligh grade from Gilbert Yard.

N&W freights also were run over this VGN line i similar fashion – at least once with an N&W Y-clas 2-8-8-2 on the point.

The entire Guyandotte River Line – employee call it "the Guyan River Line" – is slightly downgrad westbound and follows this river all the way to Gi bert Yard. For the majority of its length it is well hid den from view and is followed by West Virginia Stat Route 10.

In the mid-1970s, about the westernmost 20 mile of this branch was relocated by construction of th U.S. Army Corps of Engineers R. D. Bailey Dam fo flood control. The new line from Shannon and Bai leysville was stabbed with several stiff grades sout of the original right-of-way to Justice and Gilber which replaced the easy river alignments.

The new line also bypassed the completely isolat ed former telegraph offices at Simon and Cub Cree Junction, plus Hatfield and a few more tunnels e route.

A few steam-era derailments occurred on thi line but none were major. At least twice, a U.S. Ma let turned over into the Guyandotte, this affordin passersby a few good photos from WV Route 10 o the opposite bank of the river of steam-powered VGI Wrecking Crane B-19 hauling the big Mallets back u the bank and re-railing the massive iron hulks.

Cub Creek Branch

An approximately 10-mile-long branch was buil off VGN's Guyandotte River Line in the late 1930s t serve a major mine at Coal Mountain.

Station Number	Miles from Norfolk	Guyandot River Branch STATIONS
375	374.7	..........ELMORE..........
L381	381.2	..........JAZBO.......... 6.5
L387	386.5	..........PINEVILLE.......... 5.3
L393	392.6	..........MADA.......... 6.1
L399	398.5	..........ALIFF.......... 5.9
L402	402.0	..........SHANNON.......... 3.5
L405	405.1	..........SIMON.......... 3.1
L406	405.4	......SIMON JUNCTION...... 0.3
L411	411.0	....CUB CREEK JUNCTION... 5.6
L414	414.0	..........JUSTICE.......... 3.0
L416	415.9	........GILBERT YARD.......... 1.9
L418	418.0	..........GILBERT.......... 2.1
....	418.3	........WEST GILBERT........ 0.3

Station Number	Miles from Norfolk	Coal Mountain Branch STATIONS
L411	411.0	....CUB CREEK JUNCTION...
R416	416.0	..........BRADLEY.......... 5.0
R418	418.4	......COAL MOUNTAIN...... 2.4

Station Number	Miles from Norfolk	Morri Branch STATIONS
L406	405.4	......SIMON JUNCTION......
M413	413.0	..........PLUNKETT.......... 7.6
M415	415.2	..HUFF CREEK JUNCTION... 2.2
M417	417.0	..........OCEANA.......... 1.8
M419	419.4	..........HATCHER.......... 2.4
M425	424.7	........KOPPERSTON........ 5.3

In later years under Norfolk Southern operation, the line was considerably shortened because of the closure of that mine. Other small coal outlets on the lower end of this line are still served by NS.

A radical change in the first several miles of this line occurred in the early 1970s when the U. S. Army's Huntington District R. D. Bailey Lake project forced relocation of the western half (about 20 miles) of the Guyandotte River Line.

The original location of Cub Creek Junction was totally inaccessible by any road and was just west of Hatfield Tunnel in a sheer crevasse cut by the Guyandotte River about 30 miles west of Elmore Yard, the closest post office being Justice.

"New Cub Creek Junction" is a small part of the many-million-dollar 20 miles of new railroad built nearly 40 years ago. The new branch junction switch and passing siding was blasted deep into the hillside and is just east of one of the several tunnels on this line. This location is also just about inaccessible by road traffic.

Anyone who worked this area on a train crew 60-plus years ago would not recognize any part of the trackage!

Morri Branch

This 19.6-mile-long route from the very remote telegraph office at Simon Junction, Wyoming County, west by 31.6 miles of Elmore Yard, through Oceana and terminating at the former giant Kopperston Mine, was constructed in the late 1930s with the discovery of a new coal seam several miles north (railroad west) of the well-established community of Oceana.

Your author has talked with several VGN telegraph operators who had to walk more than two miles from the nearest dirt road to the one-room Simon Telegraph Office just to get to get to work. They also and most certainly had to look out for copperheads and rattlesnakes all along the way. I made this very walk along the Guyan River Line with my Dad in 1958.

Once there these gentlemen – one for each eight-hour shift to cover 24 hours – always had to plan to sleep and eat there for several days at a time – in the back of the quite small telegraph office. Plus there were no grocery stores, rooming houses, bathrooms, showers, radio or television for literally miles! Crowded living conditions, for sure.

The new mine – one of Virginian's newest and thus one of Virginian's last, opened in 1938, and owned and run by the Koppers Coal Company of Pittsburgh, Pennsylvania.

The company soon realized what a gem VGN was as a railroad investment and soon bought its largest single block of company stock – about 37 percent. Twenty-two years later, Koppers voted its VGN stock in favor of the Virginian-Norfolk & Western merger along with nearly all other shareholders, thus ending VGN's corporate life on December 1st, 1959.

Several smaller mines were developed along the Morri Branch (pronounced "MORE-eye") through the years but the quite deep Kopperston mine was always the largest on this route and produced more coal than nearly any other on Virginian.

A 1.4-mile-long line named Huff Creek Branch from Huff Creek Junction to Lynco, served at least one coal mine and was laid down before 1950. This is located a few miles east of Oceana.

Instead of the Morri Branch, the railway earlier planned to construct a 24.1-mile-long line to connect the coal camp of Morri, 2.4 miles west of Sabine on the subsidiary Virginia & Western Railway Branch. However, it was never constructed and the line along Clear Fork through Oceana was built up the creek from very remote Simon from a switch on the Guyan River Line.

This proposed line's use as a way to shorten some mine runs – nearly all of which operated out of Elmore yard – certainly was feasible. The never-built line would have completed a rough circle in the Wyoming County coalfields. Perhaps a good look through the company Authorities for Expenditure files in the care of the N&W/VGN Historical Society in Roanoke would reveal why it was never constructed.

Virginian Railway dieselized its coalfields nearly completely in 1954. No. 55, the sixth of the line's 25 Fairbanks-Morse Train Masters made a break-in run out to switch Kopperston mine shortly after arrival in Elmore Yard with several other units from F-M's plant in Beloit, Wisconsin.

As the engineer let his new unit start down the steep grade out of the small Kopperston mine yard, he discovered to his horror that No. 55 had no brakes. As several folks inside the nearby company store watched entranced, speed increased dramatically, especially with the weight of the loaded hoppers behind the No. 55!

The fireman "joined the birds" – jumped out of the locomotive quickly – and the brand-new No. 55 jumped the rails and fell over the cinder-and-limestone-ballasted bank and down about 30 feet.

No real harm occurred except to the crew's tem-porary sense of well being – and the Elmore wrecker and its crew had the engine re-railed in not much time at all.

Following a day or two inside Mullens Motor Barn for a very thorough inspection including help from several F-M representatives, the new unit was back at work on lots of mine runs for about the next 20 years. New brakes and new brakeshoes all around the two six-axle trucks were certainly the order of the day.

However, No. 55's first revenue run will never be forgotten, especially by the engineer and his crew!

With the passage by Congress of the 12-hour maximum Hours of Service Law in the 1970s, train and engineer service crews could not finish a mine run roundtrip through much of that rural territory in the time allotted. So N&W after the merger had built a bunkhouse for layovers for the men at Hatcher just east of Oceana. It is still in service and is certainly not as isolated as the Simon Telegraph Office had once been.

About 20 years ago, the Kopperston mine simply ran out of mineable coal and shut down. The Morri Branch may have been mothballed in the 1980s except for a very smart Norfolk Southern coal marketing officer who, in the 1990s, realized a unique opportunity – both for his company and for his own career.

A new 1970s French-owned mine was served for about 20 years by Chesapeake & Ohio and successor CSX Transportation at the very western end of the long Coal River Subdivision in Boone County, West Virginia, west out of St. Albans.

Perceiving a chance for NS to have this revenue for southbound coal, as well as to shorten the distance (and thus the freight charges) from this mine to the coal's North Carolina power plant destination, Marketing Officer Bill Bailes proposed – and NS had built – a three-mile-long conveyor belt.

Of course, CSX objected to NS' several necessary permits but all to no avail.

The all-weather covered rubber belt extends from the mine tipple near the end of CSX trackage across the very steep and rugged Bolt Mountain to a new tipple immediately east of the abandoned and original late 1930s VGN Kopperston operation! And the now retired marketing man's career looked mighty good!

Winding Gulf Branch

This 32.3-mile-long coal line was Virginian's first major branch and most of it still survives since its beginning about 1905. Construction on it started about four years before the Deepwater and Tidewater Railways were joined at Glen Lyn, Virginia, in January 1909.

Most of VGN's branch line mines were served by the Winding Gulf, which was named for the stream which begins in Raleigh County and joins with Stone Coal Creek at Amigo to form the Guyandotte River. The Guyandotte itself flows into the Ohio River next to the eastern Huntington suburb of Guyandotte.

The main section of the Winding Gulf Line extends geographically northwest from Gulf Junction at the west end of Elmore Yard past the former Mullens Motor Barn – demolished as of September, 2011 – and on to Pemberton, 25.4 miles distant.

Many colorfully-named familiar VGN locations are on this line, including Amigo, Stone Coal Junction, Helen, Stotesbury, Hot Coal, Big Stick, Pickshin, Loop Junction and Sophia. The branch then proceeds geographically west from the C&O (now CSX Transportation) interchange point at Pemberton for several miles and ends at Willabet which is on a hillside above Lillybrook and the former location of the mine at Besoco.

A 2.7 mile spur east of Fireco was the penultimate branch VGN ever built and because of the timing of its construction just after World War II was nicknamed by employees "The Burma Road" after the dangerous land and air supply route through Southeast Asia.

Winding Gulf Branch was the location of the most intense competition between VGN and C&O because many mines along that stream were jointly served by both companies. This meant the coal company had its choice of which railroad would haul its coal, a truly competitive situation which is not usually as obvious as this.

Tracks of both rail companies crossed the Winding Gulf stream at several points and each granted trackage rights to the other. This situation extends to the present day for the few mines that remain active.

About 1990, C&O got permission from the Interstate Commerce Commission to abandon much of its own Winding Gulf branch, including the Gulf Switchback, a real operational headache that even required a round-the-clock telegraph office for decades.

Station Number	Miles from Norfolk	Winding Gulf Branch STATIONS
375	374.7	..............ELMORE............
....	376.5	........GULF JUNCTION......
....	376.9	......WYE JUNCTION....... 0.4
B378	378.2	......BLACK EAGLE......... 1.3
B380	380.1	......ALLEN JUNCTION...... 1.9
B382	382.4	........STEPHENSON........ 2.3
B384	384.1	..........AMIGO.......... 1.7
B387	387.1	...........HELEN......... 3.0
B389	389.3	............TAMS.......... 2.2
B391	391.1	.......STOTESBURY........ 1.8
B392	392.2	......WOODBAY......... 1.1
B393	393.4	.......BIG STICK........ 1.2
B394	393.9	..........HOT COAL........ 0.5
B395	394.9	......LOOP JUNCTION....... 1.0
B398	397.6	..........SOPHIA......... 2.7
B399	399.1	..........AFFINITY....... 1.5
B400	400.1	........PEMBERTON........ 1.0 C. & O. RY. CROSSING
B402	402.1	..........SULLIVAN.......... 2.0
B405	404.9	..........BOWYER........ 2.8
B405.5	405.2	...........WHITBY......... 0.3
B406	406.3	..........JONBEN....... 1.1
B407	407.0	..........FIRECO.... 0.7
B410	410.0	..........WILLABET......... 3.0

Thus, only a small portion of track in that valley is now CSX and NS crews do a lot of switching and delivery of CSX coal to CSX. A newly-opened mine at Affinity – which for many years was a jointly-served mine – has its traffic delivered only five per cent to CSX and 95 per cent to NS.

A significant photograph in VGN history was taken in the vicinity of Loop Junction about 1957 by Elmore Yard Clerk O. W. "Pete" Andrews. Obviously arranged with the train crew and the Princeton dispatcher, the engineer stopped his still new Fairbanks-Morse "Train Master" locomotive several car lengths east of the Loop Junction Tunnel.

For it is here that VGN's Winding Gulf Branch, in its descent from Pemberton and Sophia to Elmore

Yard makes a distinct loop on the hillside, travels through a short tunnel and crosses over the C&O branch proceeding from Raleigh Yard near Beckley, just downhill from its own Winding Gulf Switchback.

Mr. Andrews stood on the upper segment of track closer to the caboose and took his black-and-white photograph, which depicts a most unusual scene.

His photo did not receive much attention until after the VGN-N&W 1959 merger and the shot was later featured in "Ripley's 'Believe It Or Not" Sunday comic strip.

Although not even now well-known, a fatal derailment occurred on the Winding Gulf in 1933. This was a head-on at the East Switch Amigo – four miles up the Gulf from Gulf Junction -- between the westbound local passenger train headed by a TA Class 4-6-0 and an eastbound coal drag with a 700-series Mallet up front. The veteran engineer on the passenger train was killed in the tragedy after he misread his meet order, a fatal mistake that too many railroaders made in years gone by.

One other note is a fine example of how one generation does not recall its predecessor's history very well. It is a simple street sign in the town of Helen.

Just across West Virginia State Route 16 from a substantial stone miner's memorial is a sign designating "SCRIPT ST.," a poor substitute for what should have been "SCRIP ST.," which names the early coal companies' own miners' currency!

Station Number	Miles from Norfolk	Allen Branch STATIONS
B380	380.1	......ALLEN JUNCTION......
		1.1
O381	381.2	..............WYCO..........

Station Number	Miles from Norfolk	Stone Coal Branch STATIONS
B384	384.1	...............AMIGO........
		0.5
D385	384.6	...STONE COAL JUNCTION...
		0.9
D386	385.5	...........RHODELL.........
		0.6
D386.5	386.1	...........FRANCIS.........
		1.4
D387.5	387.5	........EAST GULF.........
		1.0
D389	388.5	........KILLARNEY........
		0.9
D389.5	389.4	..........MEAD..........
		1.2
D390	390.6	..........BESOCO.........
		2.2
D393	392.8	.........LILLYBROOK........

Allen Branch

This 2.8 mile long branch off VGN's Winding Gu Branch, left that line just east of Amigo and ran u

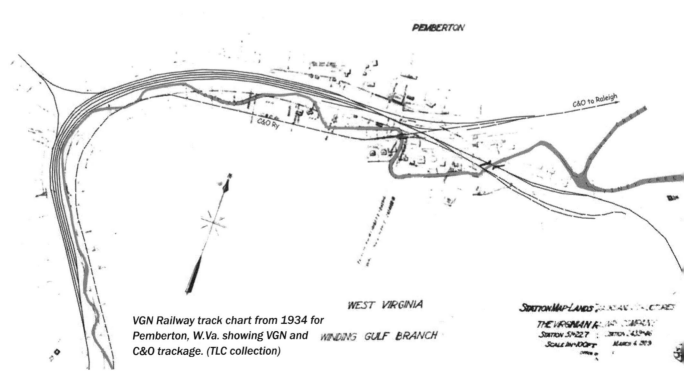

VGN Railway track chart from 1934 for Pemberton, W.Va. showing VGN and C&O trackage. (TLC collection)

llen Creek from Allen Junction to Lane, site of two ormer coal mines owned by the Wyoming Coal Company, hence the name "Wyco."

A community church erected about 100 years ago s now a major structure up this hollow. Volunteer epair crews from New York, Georgia and other locaions have been putting this old coal company church ack into first-class shape for about two years and vere brought together by a true 21st Century device the Internet.

Stone Coal Branch

From its junction with the Winding Gulf Branch t Amigo Station, this line went into a short tunnel nd then arrived at a small yard jointly shared with &O's Winding Gulf Subdivision, which ended here or many years after its 16-mile-long journey from Raleigh Yard just south of Beckley.

For the last several years, NS has gathered all he coal loads and distributed all the empty hoppers rom CSX and delivered them to the competing line t Pemberton.

Stone Coal Junction was just the beginning of this ital VGN branch line, which extended 9.1 miles furher west to Besoco and several other coal camps beore ending at Lillybrook.

Until the mid-1930s, the local first-class passenger nd mixed trains served all these branch lines. In adition, U.S. Mallets of the 700 and also Class AE 800 eries articulateds "coaled up" under the tipples they erved.

One major mine on this line was – and still is today located at East Gulf, milepost 5.

Devils Fork Branch

This short branch – now completely abandoned – an from Amigo up Devil's Fork Hollow for 1.09 miles o at least one mine.

The junction switch actually was off the Stone oal Branch to Lillybrook, making Amigo Station the unction for three branches.

As on most VGN branches – as well as C&O and &W in Southern West Virginia – various lumber ompanies also had sawmills erected along the rightsf-way. Shay-, Heisler- and Climax-powered log spurs perated throughout much of this territory and sevral were established before the Class I railroads.

Station Number	Miles from Norfolk	Devils Fork Branch STATIONS
B384	384.1	..........AMIGO..........
		1.1
....	385.2	........END OF LINE........

Station Number	Miles from Norfolk	Collins Spur STATIONS
B395	394.9	.......LOOP JUNCTION.......
		1.0
G396	395.9	.........MISTLETOE.........
		0.3
G397	396.2	.......WINDING GULF.......

These logging line railways were first laid on the ground about 110 years ago and some lasted until just after World War II.

Collins Spur

As Deepwater Railway construction men graded the right-of-way and laid tracks up Winding Gulf and met readily mineable bituminous on the way up into Raleigh County, towns like Stotesbury were established close to the brand-new mineheads.

At the west end of a short tunnel about half way to Pemberton, a 1.3 mile-long valley opened up, also the scene of C&O's Winding Gulf Switchback. Although Deepwater Railway civil engineers had determined they would complete a loop of track in order to surmount the hill into Pemberton and the initial C&O interchange in that area, the valley off to the right deserved attention as a branch line to more and more coal revenues.

Starting from a switch at Loop Junction in the western end of the tunnel, yet another new branch left the mainline and was laid on a slight grade toward the future scene of a new coal camp named Winding Gulf. The only station between Loop Junction and Winding Gulf was named Mistletoe.

Two new VGN-only mines were eventually located up this hollow but their production ended, the coal camps were demolished and tracks were removed decades ago.

This writer has seen evidence of two interesting railway operating practices at the end of the branch:

(1) Small passenger engines laid over at night and on Sundays at Winding Gulf.

(2) The larger 700-series U.S. Mallets, 800-series AE Class 2-10-10-2s, various classes of Mikados and also the passenger locomotives "coaled up" at the local tipples when necessary.

Both of the above were no doubt common throughout VGN and other road's territories.

Virginian & Western Branch

This 14.8-mile-long line, built in the early 1920's as the subsidiary Virginian & Western Railway Company for reasons unknown to this writer, marched westbound up a steep grade off VGN's mainline at V&W Junction about two miles east of the former sawmill town of Maben. V&W Junction also served as the east switch for the Maben mainline VGN/N&W/NS siding – and still does.

Although abandoned for about 25 years, the tracks are still on the ground for its route through Polk Gap Tunnel and ending at Glen Rogers, where rumors and hopes of a new coal mine to be built by a German company have surfaced for several years but that's all.

Rails have been removed from the 2.4-mile-long spur to one coal mine at Morri leading off the main V&W Branch at Sabine, just west of Polk Gap Tunnel. This could well have occurred during VGN days.

N&W and NS policies regarding abandonments differ from those of CSX, which usually tears up its tracks upon getting regulatory approval to do so, probably to avoid to paying any taxes on the property as an active railroad.

The V&W spur line never did connect with the Kopperston Branch off VGN's Guyan River Line. However, the logging roads in that area possibly did connect for a few years in the vicinity of Oceana. Both W. M. Ritter and Cole & Crane lumber companies logged over different tracts of virgin timber in this area.

What made this V&W/VGN branch line particularly fascinating was its roughly parallel 36-inch-wide logging line owned by the famous W. M. Ritter Lumber Company, once probably the largest lumber company east of the Mississippi, which merged into the giant, nationwide Georgia-Pacific Corporation in 1960.

Station Number	Miles from Norfolk	V. & W. Branch STATIONS
381	380.4	..........VIRWEST..........
V385	385.1	..........POLK GAP.......... 4.7
V390	389.4	..........MILAM.......... 4.3
V390.5	389.7	......MILAM JUNCTION...... 0.3
V395	395.2	........GLEN ROGERS........ 5.5

From the large sawmill at Maben on VGN's main line, the narrow gauge Shays slowly "churned" u[p] tough grades with their short trains of loaded an[d] empty skeleton log cars for about 20 years befor[e] VGN's V&W line was constructed.

"Over, under, around and through," the narro[w] rails seemed to show VGN the way – with seve[n] switchbacks built to conquer both sides of Polk Ga[p] Mountain while the much more modern VGN drille[d] straight through with a long tunnel there.

Much of the Ritter logging road here followed cu[t] ting over virgin timber in many parts of what is no[w] one of West Virginia's finest state parks, Twin Fall[s]. At least one other Ritter log spur – this one standar[d] gauge – overcame a steep grade to get into the Twi[n] Falls area up from VGN's "Guyan River Line" in th[e] neighborhood of the long-abandoned but "moder[n]-day" Itmann tipple.

A six-day-per-week, one-round-trip-per-day mixe[d] train served "the V&W" until the midst of The Grea[t] Depression, as well as many extra coal trains, crew[s] for which were called by call boys out of Elmore Yar[d].

The Maben sawmill was not closed and disma[n] tled until about the end of World War II, thus provi[d] ing good incomes and jobs for hundreds of famili[es] in that area for about 40 years. William M. Ritt[er] provided his employees an entire company town an[d] even a two-story brick public school.

Several of those 100-plus-year-old company hou[s] es still dot the landscape there, just like many orig[i] nal coal company houses are still providing quit[e] adequate shelter for many families in and aroun[d] Southern West Virginia.

White Oak Branch

Originally built as the 8.0-mile-long White Oa[k] Railway, what became Virginian's White Oak Branc[h] eft the Deepwater Railway mainline at a switch that as had three names: Bishop's Crossing in Deepwater Railway days, then just plain Bishop and now Oak Junction since about 1910.

Constructed about 1905 as the Deepwater Railway proceeded eastbound from Robson to Matoaka, he entire former White Oak Railway has been abandoned and the track torn up for about 15 years. This is unusual for this property as VGN, N&W and NS usually still leave tracks on the ground if there is any prospect at all of mineable coal still underground in he territory involved.

Virginian's traditional Class MB 2-8-2-powered mixed train served this line six days per week and connected with the C&O's better known "Fanny" passenger train at Oak Hill, Carlisle and perhaps one ther station. "Fanny" reached her final destination t Lester just beyond VGN's mainline.

The Oak Hill Chapter of the National Railway Historical Society did all the right things in the past few years in preserving the local station, which is a joint design by both VGN and C&O engineering departments. The group raised money to have the building ompletely rehabilitated and it simply looks great.

This structure, the former wooden freight station t Pineville on the Guyan River Line and the cinderblock signal maintainer's shanty at Matoaka are the nly two VGN stations that remain in West Virginia, 'you don't count the nearly $1 million rebuilt-from-he ground-up two-story Princeton New River Division office building plus passenger station. This was edicated Labor Day Weekend 2006.

VGN and N&W for about 65 years stationed steam

Station Number	Miles from Norfolk	White Oak Branch Northward STATIONS
418	417.7	.....OAK HILL JUNCTION....
H419	419.3	..........OAK HILL.......... 1.6
H422	421.7	.........SUMMERLEE......... 2.4
H423	423.4	.........LOCHGELLY......... 1.7
		Southward STATIONS
H419	419.3	..........OAK HILL..........
J422	421.6	..........CARLISLE.......... 2.3

and diesel-electric mine switchers in Oak Hill, the last one being the well-known "plugged-in" Train Master (VGN No. 71, which became N&W No. 171) that author and NS salesman Peter Rickershauser wrote about in a *Trains* magazine issue in the early 1970s.

"Plugged-in" means that N&W electricians at the maintenance point for the TM's at Mullens Motor Barn rigged up an ingenious electrical connection for an on-board heater on this one unit to the local Appalachian Power Company pole so the engine stayed warm at night, in winter and on weekends.

The engine facilities were immediately east of the depot and consisted of a small coal dock and water column in steam days.

Spurs west of Oak Hill depot led to both Lochgelly and Summerlee mines, no doubt youthful Irish haunts of the premier area coal operator, Justus Collins.

The area west of Elmore Yard was the last area of operation for VGN's 25 Fairbanks-Morse diesel-electrics. This writer recalls on several occasions in the early 1970s chasing triple-headed Train Masters. Photographing them crossing the high trestle at Slab Fork and also slugging it out with gravity as the combined 7,200 horsepower climbed up the original Deepwater Railway grade along Loup Creek from Deepwater to Page are sights to be remembered for a lifetime!

Also fond to this author are memories of N&W Train Master No. 171 (VGN No. 71) switching loads ("lds" in railroad terminology) and empties ("mtys") in the small yard year at Carlisle next to the local brick company store later converted to a small industry, and for several years now a private home. This was quite close to a C&O connection from Glen Jean and was at the bottom of a steep grade.

At the top of this grade was where this spur met the "mainline" White Oak Branch immediately west of the West Virginia State Route 61 grade crossing on the north side of Oak Hill. All trackage in this area is now torn up except for a short stretch near the depot for displays.

This was the vicinity of two early-days shortlines which operated independently for several years and were then leased in 1912 by VGN and C&O and then bought outright in 1917. These were the aforementioned White Oak Railway, bought by VGN, and the Piney River & Paint Creek, bought by C&O. They were both about 10-mile-long mine switching roads built by coal companies and each had its own steam locomotives, passenger cars and trains, freight and hopper cars and railroad organizations.

A third such shortline, the Kanawha Glen Jean & Eastern, was constructed as a vital operation of coal operator Samuel Dixon's New River (Coal) Company about the turn of the 20th Century. Dixon sold his approximately 20-mile-long line in 1940 to C&O.

KGJ&E connected on its west end with Virginian at the junction town of Pax, which is an interchange on the current-day West Virginia Turnpike. This line was virtually abandoned and had no traffic at all for perhaps 30 years until – in a second effort – the R. J. Corman Railroad organization of Nicholasville, Kentucky, leased it. The new company serves a single new coal "loadout" – the current name for a coal tipple – about one mile east of Pax.

However, R. J. Corman lives with a CSX stipulation in its lease agreement that it cannot interchange with NS to negotiate and obtain lower coal rates, as KGJ&E did with both VGN and C&O for about 40 years. The Corman road and NS are very close at Pax but do not join by only a few hundred yards.

The new road also serves a large woodchip mill west of Mt. Hope in Fayette County and a nearby fertilizer silo used for mixing ingredients for underground mine explosives

Shockley Branch

One of the earliest VGN shippers, dating back to early Deepwater Railway days of about 1904 was Glen White Coal Company, served by a branch 3.2 miles long, which diverted from the mainline at Glen White Junction, about 25 miles west of Elmore Yard.

This short branch was abandoned several decades ago, perhaps before the VGN-N&W merger.

The community at the west end of this mainline siding was variously known as Semoco or Metalton adjacent to West Virginia State Route 3.

On this side track shortly before World War II occurred one of VGN's 13 head-on collisions. Two U.S. Mallets met there unexpectedly, the engineer of one train named E. J. Lambert was killed.

Ingram Branch Spur

A couple miles west and down the hill toward Page and Deepwater from the nearly hidden Wriston

Tunnel is a short branch to one coal mine, Ingram Branch. This line is located across Loup Creek from West Virginia State Route 61 and is quite hard to se through decades of overgrowth.

This writer's Virginian employee father told m years ago that this spur was taken out of service an then restored when the coal company had contrac to sell coal. So it was not open at all times and I b lieve it is abandoned with the track and mine spu gone these days.

Johnson Branch

Probably less than a mile long was the Johnso Branch, which left the mainline following Johnso Fork within the village of Kincaid, just east of Page

The single bituminous coal mine on this spu played out many years ago and this author does no recall any trackage anywhere on this right-of-way.

This line dead-ended at the base of very stee Kingston Mountain, which once contained a ver productive coal seam in this immediate area.

In addition to the above noted VGN-served min C&O's Paint Creek Branch up from Hansford an Pratt on C&O's two-track mainline just west of Han ley and Montgomery ended just on the other side this hill at a coal mine named Kingston. This C& branch also has been abandoned at close to 30 year

This writer has never tried to cross that mounta but I think a four-wheeler – and a tough one at th – is required for safe passage on Fayette County Roa No. 1

Beards Fork Branch

This was Virginian's most westerly coal min branch and this line also featured the steepest grad on any part of the railway – by far.

One coal mine was at the end of this 2.6-mile-lor line and at one time its wooden tipple stretched a the way across the narrow hollow of Beards Fork an was supposed to be one of the longest in the world.

To get to this mine from Beards Junction, just ea of Robson and west of the yard at Page, VGN civ engineers and construction crews were faced with 3.48 per cent grade for about a mile.

About 10 years ago on this writer's only journe up the Beards Fork line, I observed that much trac was still on the ground, although in impassable condition without much maintenance-of-way labor and machinery. The line has not produced any revenue in perhaps 50 or more years.

However, Norfolk Southern's Coal Development Department certainly still believes that mineable bituminous in sufficient quantities to haul out of there by the trainload still exists far beneath the surface of this Fayette County hollow.

Vaco Branch

Vaco Junction did not exist before VGN contracted about 1930 to have built Deepwater Tunnel and the last bridge on the west end of the railway, the curving Kanawha River Bridge to DB Tower. This was VGN's third western connection following the mid-1930s Gilbert interchange with both C&O and N&W and the original C&O-Deepwater connection begun as the four-mile-long logging railroad formally named Loup Creek & Deepwater Railway in 1896.

This new trackage took VGN over to New York Central Railroad trackage rights. The NYC had been built about 40 years before as the Kanawha & Michigan Railroad and was the far-flung successor road NYC's most southern branch, down from Columbus, Ohio.

Vaco Junction was named for the two railways that joined at Deepwater station, "VA" for VGN and "CO" for C&O. And different sources still spell "Deep Water" variously as one word or two. VGN always spelled it as one word, including the name of its predecessor railway property.

The junction itself is all on VGN/N&W/NS property and is located one mile up the "new" track from Deepwater post office. Like a lot of locations in the Appalachian Mountains, there are no roads to Vaco Junction.

VGN's last crossing of Loup Creek proceeding westbound down from Page was curiously built of wood trestle pilings in the early 1930s. Perhaps this was an effort to meet a construction deadline and get VGN coal moving westbound as quickly as possible to all kinds of new markets in the Upper Midwestern states.

After about 70 years of service, NS forces completely rebuilt this bridge with modern concrete and steel girder construction in August, 2002.

The first westbound passenger and freight trains inaugurated this new service in 1931. Thus begun the use of NYC's Dickinson Yard in the Kanawha County town of Quincy as the western terminal for VGN freight crews – both coal and time freights.

Because of the greater number of miles on VGN from DB – which stands for "Deepwater Bridge" – Tower to Elmore yard compared with the much shorter NYC mileage from DB Tower to Dickinson Yard, freight train crews were assigned according to that ratio when calculating trackage rights and various types of operating expenses.

Thus, steel bay-window NYC cabooses were common on the cab track in the middle of Elmore Yard alongside wooden VGN Class C-1 cabs at the location many VGN men called the "Double Crossovers," also known as the West Elmore Yard Office.

The two daily passenger trains – Nos. 103-3 and 104-4 – thereafter terminated their runs at the NYC's Downtown Charleston Union Station, which also served Central first-class trains both ways from Columbus, with connections to all over the U.S.

Also at that stylish brick, two-story station there terminated trains of the Baltimore & Ohio Railroad, at one time several pairs per day running south through Central West Virginia from mainline connections throughout the U.S. at Grafton, several counties north along the Elk and rivers.

VGN's and the other railroads' locomotives were serviced overnight at the local engine house The downtown Charleston Holley Hotel was the home away from home for decades for a pair of twins, the Kelley Brothers, conductors on that pair of VGN trains.

The trains were cut back in 1952 from Charleston to Page and – with no connections whatsoever further west – this pair of "Cinder Specials" – open the windows for air conditioning! – ended for all time VGN's New River Division passenger service on July 11, 1955, with its daily turn from Page to Hales Gap, the last station stop in West Virginia.

From the earliest days of this service about 1907, VGN handed off its westbound trains to the C&O at Deepwater, running through the eastbound wye track there and the first-class passenger, express and mail cars towed backwards to the train's various terminals.

Following this handoff from VGN to C&O, VGN's steam locomotive ran light for servicing back to Page Engine House before running light again the next morning to Deepwater to pick up the eastbound train for Roanoke and – following an overnight stay – on into Norfolk, Virginia.

C&O numbered these VGN trains 32 and 33 and they variously terminated through the years at Huntington, West Virginia, and both Catlettsburg and Ashland, Kentucky. During the time of Prohibition in this country, whiskey dealers carried empty suitcases filled with empty Mason jars into Kentucky. But C&O and VGN train crews did not ask – and did not tell. If it was against federal law and the misguided constitutional amendment, they did not want to know.

On return trips, these salesmen carried full jars in full suitcases, thus giving this pair of trains the very unofficial nickname "Moonshine Specials." Surely this was not a unique operation during those years from 1918 to 1933, when these trains were discontinued. In fact, it must have been very common.

Planned But Never Constructed Branch

In the late 1950s using geological surveys, VGN's Coal Department planned and had the Engineering Department drew up plans for an approximately seven-mile-long heavy-duty mine branch from either just west of Harper or from the area around Sweeneyburg to a new property.

This proposed mine was apparently in eastern Raleigh County in the vicinity of mighty Bolt Mountain.

VGN Historian Tom Marshall, Jr., of Mullens, West Virginia, heard from his long time VGN Conductor Father Tom Marshall, Sr., and wrote this author that N&W bought out VGN on December 1, 1959, before this plan could be implemented beyond the right-of-way drawing stage.

Because of the time and talent the two companies took to efficiently merge, this proposal was temporarily shelved for several years. The plan came up again in the late 1960s as part of the much larger idea for N&W and C&O to merge themselves into what would have become the largest Eastern railroad.

This plan did not work because of the inability of C&O/B&O President Hays T. Watkins and N&W President John W. Fishwick and their staffs to agree on basics of operational, economical and political reasons.

Station Number	Miles from Norfolk	Beards Fork Branch STATIONS
430	430.3	..BEARDS FORK JUNCTION..
K433	432.9	2.6 ....BEARDS FORK........

Station Number	Miles from Norfolk	Vaco Branch STATIONS
434	434.1	.......VACO JUNCTION.......
Va. 1	435.1	1.0 ....DEEPWATER.........

At any rate, during all the negotiations in Cleveland, Roanoke and no doubt at The C&O-owne Greenbrier Hotel in White Sulphur Springs, Wes Virginia, the coal departments agreed that C&C would construct this line as an extension of its Bi Coal River Subdivision running geographically south out of St. Albans, West Virginia.

This was accomplished by C&O, the thought bein that both roads as one would share the revenues o one balance sheet. However, after the merger did no come to fruition, C&O/B&O thus got all this traffi for several decades – until an NS marketing office hit upon a very bright idea, which probably solid fied the remainder of his career. About 20 years ag NS "stole the traffic" from C&O/B&O successor CS Transportation by having built a three-mile-long heavy-duty completely covered conveyor belt fror the mine on CSX over treacherous Bolt Mountai to a new tipple immediately east and geographicall south of the by then abandoned VGN/N&W/NS Kor perston tipple built in the 1930s.

This story is also told in the Morri Branch sectior

While not an early pioneer in American or world railway electrification, The Virginian Railway and its consultant and designer Gibbs & Hills of Washington, D.C., tore into this well proven form of railroad motive power in a massive way like no other line had up to that time.

The Baltimore & Ohio installed a short route for several small electrics in 1896 as a way to get through its smoke-stifled Mount Royal Tunnel in downtown Baltimore. This was the first such installation in the world and it proved very satisfactory for several decades.

From this grew the pioneering 440-mile-long Milwaukee Road electrification in two sections across both Rockies and Bitter Root Mountains. Begun in 1911, it lasted until the railroad around it virtually collapsed in the 1970s and 1980s.

There followed the competing Norfolk & Western installation of 1915 extending from Bluefield, West Virginia, west through the McDowell County coalfields to Iaeger, about 50 miles or half way across limits of N&W's famous revenue-producing Pocahontas Division.

The best known electrification program in American history because of its metropolitan location in the Northeast was the Pennsylvania Railroad's long and extremely efficient project started in the 1920s from Washington, D. C., to New York City and – as a branch of this four-track mainline – from Philadelphia to Harrisburg, Pa.

This was partially built with Federal Government funds during the Great Depression and is the only electrically-operated line of an American railroad in the 21st Century.

European and Japanese electric schemes were the first in the rest of the world, dating from the 1930s or so, with the Chinese railway construction of very high speed train routes run by electric locomotives coming on the railroad scene only within the past 10 years.

Thus, we come to The Virginian which, as I noted in my general introduction to this book, may never have ventured into electric traction for its freight service except for the problems steam crews had on Clarks Gap Mountain. This lasted from the beginning of service about 1905 until the long and bitter strike for several months in 1923.

Three very different classes of electric locomotives were eventually employed to haul VGN coal, empties and time freights the 136 miles from Mullens, West Virginia, to Roanoke, Virginia, and back. This motive power was very definitely from three different generations and two builders, one class looking nothing at all like the previous or successor models.

The first two were considered the largest and most powerful engines of their type anywhere. The third set used many parts that were interchangeable with those used on existing diesel-electric locomotives, and were notable for their ignitron rectifier power plants.

Upon their introduction in 1956-57, railroad executive John W. Barriger said he considered these 12 locomotives as some of the best freight engines ever built.

Because Southern West Virginia and the involved part of Southwestern Virginia were considered pretty much of a backwater for electricity in the 1920s, Virginian management contracted with several firms to install its electrification scheme and the 75-foot-or-so-tall transmission towers to feed the catenary wires.

Most important was to provide the supply of electricity in sufficient quantities to operate the locomotives pulling up the several on-line grades, and to allow the engines to "give back" power from the motors in regenerative mode while descending those grades.

Following the lead of competitor N&W, Virginian and Gibbs & Hill found just the right location on the shallow and beautiful New River within the town of Narrows, Virginia, to construct a large two-stack power plant to produce the necessary 11,000 volts of A.C. power.

Water from the north-flowing river was taken into the plant's basement where boilers produced steam to turn the four large generators to produce the power. This was the electricity that my father told me to stay away from at all costs.

Oh, those locomotives – the 36 individual "squareheads" of the mid-1920s – I've also heard them called "flatheads;" the four stylish and just beautiful "streamliners" (or "roundnoses") of 1948; and the 12 "rectifiers" of 1956-57, which I never heard called "bricks" until recent railfan-inspired nicknames came into vogue – for some. (These must be the same folks who wrongly call VGN's 120-ton-capacity gondolas "battleship" gons, which most VGN employee ever used.)

Bigger, mightier and stronger than any form of locomotive ever used to pull trains on rails anywhere in the world were the massive three-unit Class EL-3A jack-shaft locomotives produced in 36 separate units by Westinghouse Electric & Manufacturing Company of suburban Pittsburgh, Pennsylvania. They served all over the electrified territory until No. 113, the last active unit, was pulled from service on Halloween of 1959, tying up on a work train in front of the Princeton depot. Interestingly, some crewman had neatly lettered the word "CLARABELLE" in all capital letters on her pilot.

Featured in many advertisements in railway trade journals and some in the popular newspaper press of the day, two sets (or six units) of these true giants of the rails easily beat a similar weight and length steam-powered coal drag from Elmore Yard to Clarks Gap Summit, despite that fact that the steam train – with a 600-series Class AD 2-8-8-2 steam giant on the head end and two 800-series Class AE 2-10-10-2 leviathans pushing in front of the wooden caboose – was given a lead.

By the time the pair of well-publicized coal drags reached Garwood Bridge, about half way up Virginian's stiffest mainline grade, the electric train was already clearly the winner!

The jack shaft drive's most obvious outward feature was that its side rods – which looked for all the world just like those on a steam locomotive – acted just like the steam engine's rods as they flailed around the diameter of the wheels.

These units also rode and felt just like steam locomotives, though, of course, their resemblance was much closer to the developing diesel-electrics. The author had one chance to ride one of these beasts when my friend and Head Brakeman John Henry Smith invited me to hop aboard No. 100, which was then operating as two (instead of the usual three) units as we headed through the east end of Princeton Yard to pick up eastbound Local Freight No. 64 bound for Roanoke one Saturday morning about summer of 1957.

In my single Class EL-3A ride of only about one-half mile, No. 100 rode like a Mallet to me, slowly heaving from side to side as the rods counterbalanced each other down the yard track.

After World War II and the wear and tear of two decades of virtually continuous use, VGN managers wanted something to replace the "squareheads," at least partially. Along came four of the most stylish electrics of that day and time, looking a lot like the new streamlined carbodies of General Motors' early E and F series passenger and freight diesel-electric locomotives that were then rolling out of GM's Electric-Motive Division La Grange, Illinois, shop.

Below and Right: Map and profile of the Virginian electrified district. (Lloyd D. Lewis collection)

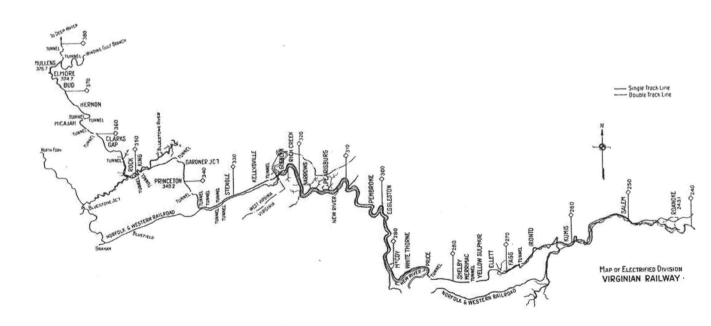

However, General Motors had little experience in building electric locomotives so the job went to General Electric's relatively new shop in Erie, Pennsylvania. One at a time in the early months of 1948 the four million-pound monsters left the shop and were individually tested on GE's special long test track.

Impressive like no other locomotives that workaday, blue collar, coalfields culture VGN had even considered buying, upon arrival a month apart in 1948 at the Mullens Motor Barn (demolished in 2011), they were immediately dubbed what else but "Streamliners" by VGN men.

As discussed elsewhere in this text, the Class EL-2Bs were true "giants of the rails," dwarfing all other locomotives – and even many buildings -- in sight.

They performed flawlessly, doing everything they were designed for – and could have nearly reached their top design speed of 52 m.p.h. However, probably not anywhere in West Virginia – only perhaps on the locally famous "Salem Flats" west of that Roanoke County, Virginia, county seat. Here steam-powered eastbound VGN freights were known to have "bested by a long shot" N&W passenger trains just a few feet away, according to H. Reid's text.

The 125's big test run that first winter operated from the Motor Barn to Roanoke Yard Office, pulling only the office car "Guyandotte River" filled with the railway's top executives and a wooden caboose with crew.

Performance of the EL-2B No. 125 was all spectacular, Tom Marshall reported, on one of his first official runs as possibly the newest VGN brakeman – the proud new man on the crew.

Eight years later, further wear and tear on those old reliable 36 EL-3A units caused management to order 12 unprecedented electric locomotives – this time also from General Electric in Erie, Pennsylvania. The first pair arrived in late 1956 and the remaining 10 "coming on line" in 1957.

These last VGN electrics were classed EL-C, keeping in mind George Byron Halstead's original scheme of simple classifying and numbering of all rolling stock that he had devised about 1907 when he and wife Nancy arrived to live in Princeton for almost the rest of his life.

As part of their modern power plants, the new locomotives contained ignitron rectifiers, which made them more powerful as well as more efficient in operation on those West Virginia Hills. This new-fangled technology worked fine and pulled heavy coal trains up and over Clark's Gap Mountain just great.

This author's father, W. G. Lewis, who was Virginian's final Supervisor of Telegraph and Signals, knew of the rectifiers in ways that he would rather not have known. The rectifier's – the EL-Cs official nickname – not "bricks" – only major flaw caused serious interferences with the railway's telephone communications, producing a very audible hum on the

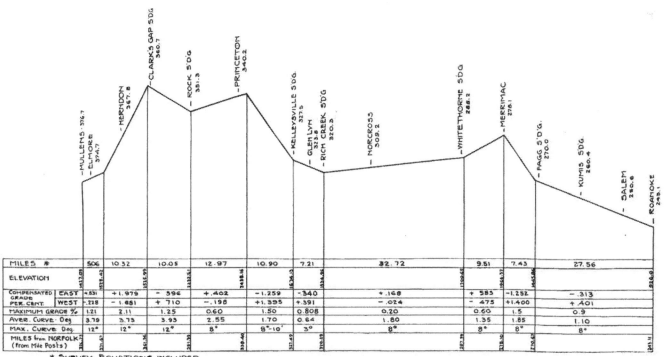

Condensed Profile of the Electrified Section

A 6800-HP ELECTRIC LOCOMOTIVE

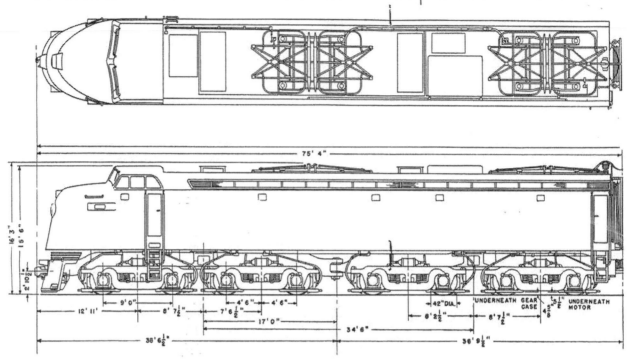

PRINCIPAL DATA

Wheel Arrangement	- - -	2 [(B-B) + (B-B)]
Total Weight	- - -	1,000,000
Weight on Drivers	- - -	1,000,000
Number of Driving Axles	-	16
Weight per Driving Axle	-	62,500 lbs
Continuous Rating		
At Rail	- - -	6,800 hp
Tractive Effort	- -	162,000 lbs
Speed	- - -	15.75 mph
Adhesion	- -	16.2 per cent
Starting Tractive Effort		
26% Adhesion	- -	260,000 lbs

Maximum Operating Speed	- - -	50 mph
Number of Traction Motors	- -	16
Gear Ratio	- - -	70 17
Line Voltage	- - -	11,000
Phases	- - -	Single
Cycles	- - - -	25
Air-Brake Equipment		Type 8 EL straight and automatic
Number of Compressors	- -	4
Compressor Air Capacity	- -	600 cfm
Type of Control	- -	PCL Electro-Pneumatic
Maximum Track Curvature Operable	-	19 Degrees

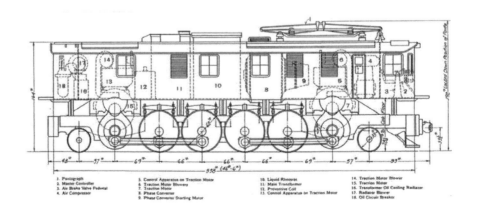

These drawings show the three types of VGN electric locomotives, all to the same scale. (Lloyd D. Lewis collection)

WITH A MILLION POUNDS ON DRIVERS

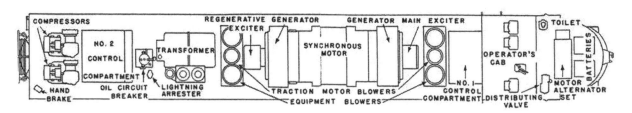

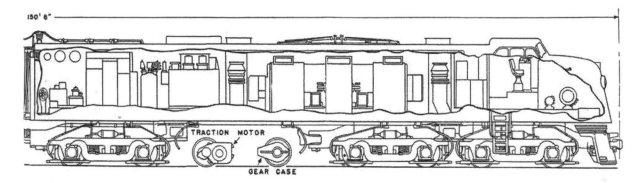

AND DIMENSIONS

Length Overall, between Knuckles	150 ft 8 in
Total Wheel Base	133 ft 8 in
Rigid Wheel Base	9 ft
Width Overall	11 ft 1 in
Height over Pantograph, Locked Down	16 ft 3 in
Driving Wheel Diameter	42 in
Height over Cab	15 ft 6 in
Width over Handrails	11 ft 1 in
Width over Cab	10 ft 4 in
Track Gage	4 ft 8½ in
Coupler Height	2 ft 10½ in
Clearance over Rail, New Wheels	4⅝ in

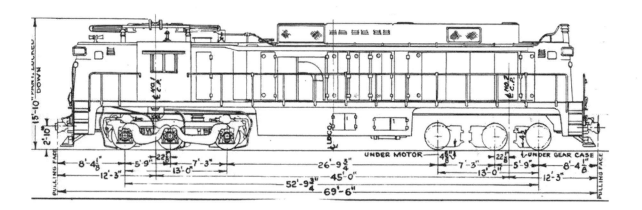

lines. After a couple years or so, this not only annoying but potentially dangerous situation was finally solved and even involved at least one unit equipped with a device on its side near its top.

But little did this matter in the "Big Scheme of Virginian Things". The railway itself was corporately "done in" only one minute after Midnight on the first day of December 1959.

And then the entire electrification scheme itself predictably was taken out of service as a "one-way operation" on Saturday night, June 30, 1962, and was then soon thereafter scrapped and the remaining locomotives either scrapped or sold on the cheap.

One of this writer's earliest memories of "life on the railroad" with my dad was walking down several iron stairs into the very bowels of the seemingly gigantic Narrows Power Plant. Several times there I watched him fill up five-gallon glass bottles with distilled water drained from the bottoms of the four huge coal-fired boilers.

These boilers every day efficiently burned five 50-ton-capacity VGN hoppers full of "West Virginia real estate." They thus produced high-pressure steam to turn the four turbine generators that powered "our locomotives," as my Dad frequently told me.

These glass bottles were for Dad's use in large Edison storage batteries located in on-line signal bungalows at the ends of each signaled siding and at some gate-and-flasher-protected grade crossings. These batteries assured back up power for the proper functioning of these various signals in case the local Appalachian Power went off in storms.

A truly very important milestone in my youth occurred at just about 8 p.m. on Saturday night, June 30, 1962, when Dad and I were the only non-working railroaders attending the formal shutdown of the 37.5-year-old Narrows Power Plant.

This sad occasion – "we railroaders" all had stiff upper lips, that night, for sure – happened just a few days following N&W top management in Roanoke deciding it could no longer use VGN's essentially "one-way electrification scheme."

N&W Railway officers had tried – and tried hard – to work Virginian's grand plan – which had made VGN's entire operations a nearly unbelievable 45 percent more efficient mostly single-track run from about 1925 on – into their newly dieselized two-track mainline on the opposite side of the New River for

many miles through Southwestern Virginia – but a to no avail.

Just after 8 p.m. that early summer night, wor was received from the South Roanoke yardmaste that the final electric-powered train – Time Freigh No. 72 of that day with Engineer Emory S. Whit at the throttle – had arrived in the designated yar track and stopped, pantographs down.

The three nearly new EL-C GE engines stayed jus about where they were in South Roanoke Yard fc several months and were sold several months late with the other nine to the New Haven Railroad an shipped dead-in-tow to Cedar Hill Yard in New Ha ven, Connecticut.

But back to the real and nearly silent drama wit nessed by only my dad, this writer and four other rai road men, including General Foreman and Virginia Company Photographer George King Shands on hi very last night of work at 62 years old.

As his last official act in his many-year career, Sec ond Trick Power Director Charles C. Linkenhoker c Narrows twisted the two-foot-long handle on the las operating steam turbine.

Then everything got very quiet up there in th top-floor General Foreman's chambers as we listene to the turbine slowly, ever so slowly, grind to a fina halt. By shortly before 9 p.m., it was all over – an about 50 men had lost their careers and had take their retirements – or, as we railroaders, say, "pulle the plug."

However, in a real twist of irony, the opposite thin occurred to your author the very next day. At my ter der age of 16, during that afternoon following churcl at our home on Park Avenue about 30 miles west i Princeton, I was writing up my notes on the previou evening's events. It was exactly at this very time tha I decided to become a writer!

The Motor Barn at Mullens was the primary service location for the VGN electric fleet. This view of the back shows EL-3A squareheads and EL-2B streamliners parked on storage tracks awaiting assignment to eastbound trains on June 18, 1949. (Richard J. Cook photo, Lloyd D. Lewis collection)

The class (or first numbered) locomotive of the EL-3A "Squareheads," No. 100, sits at the end of a stub track behind the Motor Barn. West Virginia State Route 16 is on the hillside behind the 100, which was turned out in a Pittsburgh suburb in 1923. These were the first three of 36 individual units constructed over the next three years. No certain date. (Malcolm McCarter collection)

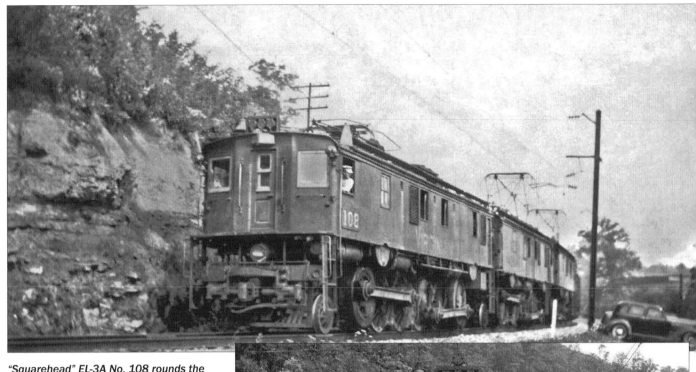

"Squarehead" EL-3A No. 108 rounds the Princeton Shops Crossing curve with an eastbound coal drag in 1947. (H. Reid Photo, Lloyd D. Lewis collection)

Squarehead No. 103 and several fellow units are parked temporarily out of service in the rear of Mullens Motor Barn. No certain date. (Malcolm McCarter collection)

One of the 36 EL-3A units sits outside the Mullens Motor Barn for a photograph of definite ungainliness. These engines sure looked better from the front end in one-, two- and three-unit lashups. No certain date. (Malcolm McCarter collection)

Big electric No. 105 is parked in back of the Motor Barn in April 1956 with those huge steam-type rods very visible. The humble miner's home at top left has been around since before the Motor Barn in 1923. In the early days of the 21st Century, it is nearly totally fallen down and gone – like the Motor Barn itself. (Jim Shaw Photo, Lloyd D. Lewis collection)

Emphasized by the bright and original wall of glass construction of the Mullens Motor Barn, EL-3A No. 111 sits after her latest overhaul inside this building. No. 111 was, until December, 1941, three separate units, which were used for local service for approximately the first 15 years of their existence. No definite date. (Ben F. Cutler photo, Lloyd D. Lewis collection)

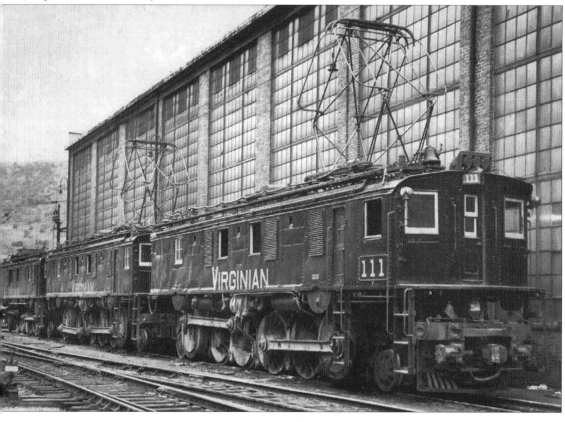

In August 1955, Jack Shaft No. 105 is flanked by a single-unit EL-1A between the dual sand towers and the east side of the now demolished Mullens Motor Barn. (John Patrick Killoran photo, Lloyd D. Lewis collection)

Rear end of EL-1A No. 113 parked in front of the Mullens Motor Barn. Date not certain. This unit was later lettered "CLARABELLE" in reference to the television clown of the 1950s, the name appearing on the pilot on the unit's other end. No. 113 was also the last of the EL-3A engines ever in service and was retired from work train service on Halloween 1959, about as close to the N&W merger as possible. (Lloyd D. Lewis collection)

This print was made from a late 1920s or even earlier negative taken by the late Leonard W. Rice of Washington, D.C. Four complete sets of EL-3As are staged in back of the brand new Mullens Motor Barn. Please note the very fresh excavation from the track around the motor barn – which formed a leg of the Mullens Wye – up to what may be a new alignment of West Virginia State Route No. 16 from Mullens up the Winding Gulf to Beckley. (Leonard W. Rice Photo, Lloyd D. Lewis collection)

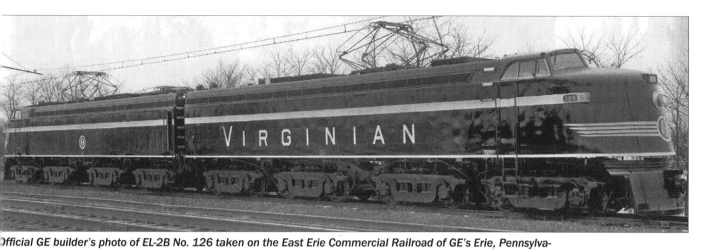

Official GE builder's photo of EL-2B No. 126 taken on the East Erie Commercial Railroad of GE's Erie, Pennsylva-nia, locomotive plant. (Lloyd D. Lewis collection)

A General Electric artist's conception of what Virginian's only really stylish and streamlined locomotives would look like upon completion in early 1948. In this view the styling bears a strong resemblance to the New Haven EP-4 and EF-3 locomotives that GE had built in 1938 and 1943, respectively. This drawing of the future Class EL-2B Nos. 125-128 was made about 1946 and appeared in both the February 1946 Railroad Magazine *and the Norfolk (Virginia)* Ledger Dispatch. *(Lloyd D. Lewis collection)*

-2B No. 127 smooth-rolls upgrade past e Kellysville, West rginia, electrification bstation and water nk hauling west-und Time Freight . 71. About summer 48. (Ben. F. Cutler oto, Lloyd D. Lewis llection)

Absolutely brand new VGN EL-2B No. 125 shines her huge bulk between the double sand towers in front of the Mullens Motor Barn probably shortly after delivery in February 1948 from the General Electric plant in Erie, Pennsylvania. The man at left appears to be VGN Chairman of the Board George D. Brooke. This author tends to believe this photo was taken on the day of it first run with VGN Office Car "Guyandotte River" and a wooden caboose from here to Roanoke. (Photo possibly taken by VGN Yard Clerk O. W. "Pete" Andrews, Lloyd D. Lewis collection)

The only streamlined locomotives of any type VGN ever owned were the four EL-2Bs GE Giants, which were probably built that way because of the newly designed diesel-electric carbodies in both freight and passenger services throughout the U.S. in the late 1940s. What a sight to behold behind the Mullens Motor Barn, especially when posed next to the angular "squareheads" of the generation just behind it right. April 1956. (Jim Shaw Photo, Lloyd D. Lewis collection)

N&W renumbered VGN Class EL-C "Rectifier" electric No. 233 and two following mates passing east end of Princeton with eastbound No. 72. VGN practice was to use two EL-C units at the head of a train but N&W began using an additional unit immediately after merger. Freight depot and New River Division office building in far left background. Winter 1960. (Lloyd D. Lewis Photo)

The last new VGN motive power is ready for action in front of the Mullens Motor Barn on May 5, 1957. EL-C 137 coupled (and usually used with) the 136 poses next to DE-RS Fairbanks-Morse Train Master No. 54. (C. K. Marsh Photo, Lloyd D. Lewis collection)

Westbound empty hoppers are being forwarded from Sewalls Point coal piers to Elmore classification yard behind new class EL-C rectifier electrics No.s 135 and 136 about 1958. The location is just west of Matoaka, Mercer County, specifically approaching the bridge at the coal camp named Giatto. (Lloyd D. Lewis collection)

Some of the world's largest and most powerful steam, electric, and diesel-electric motive power roamed the rails of The Virginian Railway from 1905 through November 30, 1959. This was particularly true on the nearly 20 coal mine branches and spurs that serviced the many mines and tipples producing this valuable product in four southern West Virginia counties.

From Baldwin C-class Consolidation 2-8-0s in four classes to the huge ALCO Class AE 2-10-10-2 Mallets, Virginian made excellent use of 213 steam locomotives, 56 electric units and 66 diesel-electric locomotives during its relatively short history, repairing them in the only large shop on the system at Princeton, West Virginia.

Starting with dozens of Mikados, the Motive Power Department in Princeton "graduated" to 500 series Class AA hand fired 2-6-6-0s, then bought from Baldwin a 2-8-8-2 No. 600, which was the world's largest when built in 1910. Then the company went back to more 2-6-6-0s for a total of 12.

Definitely one of the most interesting features of these earliest Baldwin 12-drivered mountain maulers was the requirement that they be serviced by two firemen – one left-handed and one right–handed. All these 2-6-6-0s lasted until the end of 1933, so can you imagine how "in shape" these firemen were.

According to a note written by veteran Motive Power and Mechanical Department VGN man and historian George B. Halstead, now in this author's collection, his railway considered buying large Lima Locomotive Works Shays to conquer Clarks Gap.

Actually, this would have been right in line with VGN's philosophies of buying the largest and best. Besides that, both C&O and N&W employed great big Shays to conquer stiff grades.

However, instead of geared engines, VGN first tried a noble experiment that really never worked and, at the same time, she became one of the least photographed locomotives on record.

The No. 700, designated Class XA for "experimental" in all VGN records and diagrams, had a unique wheel arrangement of 2-8-8-8-4. This leviathan of a locomotive was completed in December 1916 in Baldwin's gigantic shops in the Philadelphia suburb of Eddystone. And the 700 certainly was intended as the solution for VGN's "Clarks Gap Problem." The huge iron experiment arrived in Roanoke in December 1916 and was sent westbound dead to Elmore Yard. Quite a Christmas present!

The first locomotive engineer this author ever met, Bruce M. Bohon, a 50-year VGN man who lived in West Salem, Virginia, his entire 96-year life, recalled in an interview in December 1993 that he had witnessed the 700 being hauled very cautiously and ever so slowly dead-in-tow. This was across the interesting skewed bridge that VGN had built about 10 years before over N&W's mainline east of Kumis and west of Wabun, Virginia.

Baldwin sent several technical experts down to Elmore for testing, which involved building a shelter on the pilot for men to ride in, conducting various types of tests. However, as H. Reid espouses in his 1961 Kambach Publishing Company book *The Virginian Railway*, the monster virtually ran out of steam on its very first try-out trip, up the moderate grade from Princeton Yards to the west portal of Oney Gap Tunnel, only a mile or so eastbound of the depot and New River Division headquarters building.

However, after five quite frustrating years of literally running out of steam because the boiler did not have the necessary capacity to turn three sets of eight driving wheels, the "Noble Triplex Experiment" ended. Although it was deemed an expensive failure for Baldwin, it was one that proved its worth to both the present and the future of steam locomotive history.

From December 1916 through 1921, Triplex XA No. 700 slugged on up Clarks Gap Grade. However, it spent entirely too much time for everyone involved being tinkered with all over while stalled dead on the 2.07 per cent grade mountainside, inside the back shop at Princeton, in the Elmore Steam Shop and in dead storage in Princeton Roundhouse.

But at no other time was this non-use more significant than following the horrible winter of 1917-18. This was when Mr. Halstead told this author that, because the big loco was far too long to fit into one of the 18 conventional length Princeton roundhouse stalls, its rear end literally frozen to the rails.

And even though VGN was paying nothing at all for the big loco – and presumably did not until 1921 – several of the company's talented men, including both mechanical and locomotive engineers, plus a whole host of other trades, were occupied probably fulltime on what was virtually coming to nothing in a strictly practical sense.

Finally, the company's motive power men in Princeton and Elmore and the Baldwin Locomotive Works officers and expert mechanics from Philadelphia and Eddystone agreed that enough was really enough.

Thus, the Big Lady was hauled by a most circuitous route back to Eddystone and was cut into two separate and themselves very successful steamers which both served on Elmore Yard and beyond until the end of steam in about the mid-1950s.

These two were No. 410, a 2-8-2 and the only Class MD, which served its masters well for many years in all types of freight services and was retired and done away with in the mid 1950s like its iron horse stable mates. Then came the 610, a 2-8-8-0 which was the only Class AF. After running as a 2-8-8-0 in freight service for the next 21 years, Princeton Shops men added a two-wheel trailing truck in 1942 under the cab of the 610. This enabled it to serve as the Elmore Yard Hump Engine until that was removed in 1950 to accommodate a large expansion of classification tracks. More traffic again was the reason. The 610 is probably the only locomotive in U.S. history to have had three wheel arrangements: (1) the rear end of the one-of-a-kind 2-8-8-8-4 Triplex No. 700, (2) a rare 2-8-8-0 and (3) the singular 2-8-8-2.

As this author has stated before, almost all Virginian motive power – except its 21 0-8-0 steam switchers and all small diesel-electrics – was designed for the supreme task of their careers: Climbing Clark Gap Mountain.

This is still the toughest mainline grade on th former VGN and, except for the currently out-of-se vice but still on the ground four-per-cent-plus Salud Grade on the former Southern Railway in Wester North Carolina, may be the steepest mainline grad on all of the present Norfolk Southern's vast rail sy: tem.

Clarks Gap starts right at the east end of Elmor Yard in Wyoming County and continues until th locomotives pop out of the east portal of Algonqui Tunnel, approximately 14 miles eastbound. Grad encountered reached 2.07 per cent for a few mile meaning a rise of more than two feet for every 10 feet ahead.

Management and its civil engineers and constru tion men attempted lots of plans to successfully con quer Clarks Gap. These included larger and muc more powerful steam locomotives, double-tracking i by the early 1920s, a staff signal system of manne towers in about five locations for more efficient o erations and, finally, massive electrification for 13 miles all the way from Mullens Motor Barn to Roa noke, Virginia, accomplished between 1923 and Se tember 1926.

Plans are still extant that show Princeton motiv power folks drew plans – some probably fantasizin – for several steamers of wheel arrangements of 2-1(10-10-10-6 and possibly even larger!

A member of author H. Reid's favorite VGN locom tive type — the MB Class No. 429. This one is just east of Princeton Shops Mechanical Department just after getting her last overhaul and new paint on boiler, domes, piping, stac and feedwater heater. Sur looks nice! The smoke sta screen was most unusual on VGN steam locomotive; October 7, 1956. (Steve P: terson photo, Lloyd D. Lew collection)

The worst working conditions on the entire railway were the direct result of Clarks Gap Mountain's grade. These conditions, as discussed previously, ruined for a while some of the best labor relations between the several unions and VGN management.

A small number of originally single-track tunnels in Clarks Gap Mountain, some measuring hundreds of feet long, including Micajah nearly to the top, could not be avoided by Henry Huddleston Rogers' first-rate civil engineers and track builders

These long, dark one-track holes in the hills caused train and engine crews to suffer near-death suffocation every working day as the backed-up black coal smoke, hot cinders and scalding steam really forced the crews heading for whatever cover they could find within or outside their miserable engine cabs.

That is, until a strike by these fed-up, exhausted, tearful and very angry men. Their prolonged walkout shut down the entire VGN lines in 1923 and quickly and directly resulted in the company's board of directors approving an approximately $10 million electrification for the 136 mile-long route from the west end of Mullens (Elmore Yard) to the east end of Roanoke Yard.

As noted heretofore in this text, this huge electrification project – the largest single infrastructure project in VGN history – improved by an astounding 28 per cent the efficiency of the entire railway property – and did this immediately. Thus, we see that very good things can certainly result from very bad causes.

As the years advanced and the electrification proved to be such an obviously outstanding and astounding success, the company's profits allowed the board of directors to follow the Motive Power Department's advice and begin modernizing its fleet of coal haulers.

But in 1918, with electrification still years in the future, VGN received its first new steam power in five years – the 10 huge Class AE 2-10-10-2s from ALCO's Schenectady Works. The following year, under United States Railway Administration (USRA) control, VGN was allocated 5 2-8-8-2s, (really N&W design) numbered 900-904, which it refused, and which were subsequently sent to N&W. Later that year the road had a change of heart and accepted the first of an eventual group of 35 USRA pattern 2-8-8-2 Mallets, the second time VGN had turned to that wheel arrangement, since the pioneering Class AB No. 600.

This total of 35 VGN Class USA and Class USB 2-8-8-2 Mallets – naturally much improved versions of the pioneering No. 600 of nine years before – were delivered beginning in 1919 for the first batch of 20, which were allocated to the VGN by the WW I era USRA. The remaining 15, the USBs, were delivered four years later in 1923, and were essentially copies of the earlier USRA pattern engines.

Still literally up against the Clarks Gap problem – really getting harder to deal with day by day because of the constant yet blessed increase in eastbound coal traffic – motive power men gained approval of Norfolk Headquarters to purchase those 35 ALCO Rich-

The Princeton Yard Second Shift Yard Trick's VGN Class MB No. 443 is the subject of this H. Reid photo taken in July 1949. We all know that the MB was "Aitch's" favorite Virginian locomotive – but does anyone know why? Yes, the always colorful H. liked the "milk-can extensions" — a term he originated, this writer believes — on the cylinders designed by our friend George Byron Halstead. (H. Reid Photo, Lloyd D. Lewis Collection)

Class XA Triplex No. 700, a Baldwin product delivered in December, 1916, was a spectacular failure, whose boiler was unable to supply sufficient steam for its three sets of cylinders. Seen here in her unfortunately usual situation – out of steam on Clarks Gap Mountain, while six Baldwin and VGN men ponder how to get her going again. She probably ran out of steam more times than she made a successful pusher run on either Clarks Gap Mountain or the short grade up to Oney Gap Tunnel just east of Princeton. (George B. Halstead collection)

AF class 2-8-8-2 No. 610 is the remnant of the Triplex, consisting of the boiler and front two engines of the infamous beast. After No. 700 was returned to the builder, it was split up into this engine, originally a 2-8-8-0, and MD class 2-8-2 No. 410. VGN later added a trailing truck making the engine a 2-8-8-2, its third wheel arrangement. The engine is seen here at Elmore in June, 1950. (Lloyd D. Lewis collection)

mond coal-burning monsters to completely change its west end locomotive fleet.

But it was not that simple: At least one brand new 2-8-8-2 was photographed as VGN No. 900 before its group of locos was soon sold to neighboring N&W. We know that VGN No. 900 did not come along until 1945 as the first of the eight superbly C&O-designed 2-6-6-6s were built by Lima and came on line for service east of Roanoke to Sewalls Point for far too few years – and their scrapping by N&W in January 1960.

Why did VGN turn down the first shipment of heavy USRA 2-8-8-2s offered in 1919? We will – at this very late date – probably never know the real reasons. Besides that, personal feelings could have been involved in a situation like this and certainly may not have been written down in the company's archives so thankfully saved by the N&W Historical Society in Roanoke. But this writer has thoughtfully surmised that the cause may have been simple professional jealousy because the Mallet monsters were designed and first built by competing N&W in Roanoke.

VGN's top officers easily could have thought its own men could have done a better job of designing its own engines. However, this time that was not to be because the little line needed power a lot more than it apparently may have needed to save its own face. This author really wishes he could have discussed this years ago with someone but all those sources have been gone for probably 50 years.

New Virginian steam locomotives were necessary in the early 1920s for two good reasons:

(1) The road was now dealing with more and more eastbound coal for the furnaces of electricity generating plants in its sales territory, mainly in the Northeastern U. S. and across the oceans, but also for production of steel for the "Roaring Twenties" building booms in so many countries.

(2) The other reason was the production of much heavier and far greater capacity coal carrying rolling stock in the form of 2,025 120-ton-capacity steel construction gondolas built by the Pressed Steel Car Company in a Pittsburgh suburb, monster cars that could, in a few instances, actually outlast the railway into the early 1960s.

These cars were classed as G-3s and G-4s because they really were gondolas, not hoppers, having no open hopper bottoms for coal to be dumped out. They were also so large and heavy that they very rarely ran offline because even main tracks of these other railroads just could not take the pounding. By the way, the most coal that VGN could haul in a single carload was 50 tons up to the early 1920s.

One more note about the steepness of Clarks Gap Grade: At up to 2.07 per cent grade for a few of the 14 miles eastbound up from Elmore Yard, VGN was able to conquer the steepest but shortest route to the mountain top of the three Pocahontas Roads (N&W, C&O, and VGN). This was laid down in the first decade of the Twentieth Century

N&W was the next most severe and longest with a maximum grade of approximately 1.5 per cent eastbound for 100 miles from Williamson Yard the entire length of its original Pocahontas Division to the top of Bluefield Mountain under the Mercer Street Bridge in the middle of downtown.

This is a very rare photo of what all 10 Class AE oversized monsters looked like in preparation for shipment from the builder over several "foreign railroads" that did not have VGN's generous clearances, which were always some of the least restrictive in the world. Steam and sand domes, the large cab and the two huge high-pressure-steam front-end cylinders had to be removed after final assembly and photography and placed in a preceding gondola for the quite slow delivery trip south from the Schenectady Works of American Locomotive Company 1918. This was nothing new for VGN power, some of the largest — EVER! (American Locomotive Company Photo — John S. Aardema collection)

Giant Class AE No. 805 is in for heavy repairs on a roundhouse track east of Princeton Shops. At this time, the 805 was probably running daily coal drags to Sewalls Point from Roanoke and empties back westbound. These quite successful 2-10-10-2 behemoths were VGN's most underrated and underappreciated locomotives, in this author's opinion. No certain date. (George T. Strong, Jr. collection)

The toughest part of the N&W's climb up was along the upper reaches of the Tug Fork River from about the Farm coal dock and water spouts – where pushers are added to this day – through Welch, Keystone, Maybeury and Bluefield, Virginia, about 30 miles into Bluefield – or about 30 percent of the entire division. Most of this hill climb is in McDowell County. W.Va.

On the other hand, C&O, which had first choice of all, was surveyed and built in the early 1870s across West Virginia by men in the employ of very wealthy financier Collis Potter Huntington. From Ronceverte about 10 miles to the top of the grade about four miles east of White Sulphur Springs, the uphill measurement did not exceed 0.57 per cent, minor indeed compared with N&W and VGN.

On through the great traffic increases, rate hikes and prosperity of the Roaring Twenties – then came the 1930's and The Great Depression. Traffic dwindled to post-World War I lows, many coal mines shut down or curtailed production, laying off miners, passengers stayed away from VGN and other railroads' trains in droves, and men were laid off in shops, on the road and in the offices for the duration.

VGN was only able to pay stock dividends through the 1930s because of these layoffs and the storage of older locomotives and other rolling stock, mainly in the 18-track yard at Princeton. Out-of-service wooden coaches and wooden box and stock cars lined the tracks in all seasons for as many as three years.

Also on the deadlines were the Class MA 2-8-2s, VGN's first of that type, some of the Class EA 4-4-0s and Class TA 4-6-0s, and early Mallets – the Class AA and Class AC 2-6-6-0s, the Class AB No. 600 and perhaps others.

Then came the word from Norfolk to the Motiv Power Department: As of December 31st, 1933, reti the majority of rolling equipment stored on Princeto Yard. Never was there another date like this in Vi ginian Railway history. Entire classes of unused an worn-out equipment were stricken from the books i one day. Scrapping by several recycled metal deale occurred in 1934 and soon thereafter.

After several years of skeleton employment an depressed earnings, the railroads and most other i dustries and businesses started coming back. The Pearl Harbor Day on December 7, 1941 – and th world changed again, ever so swiftly. Train and e gine service crews, section men, telegraph operato and office workers still living in VGN territory wer rehired from almost always lower-paying jobs an mines reopened systemwide.

In the office of Car Distributor Amos R. Beam, o the second floor of the Princeton Station, orders f empty hopper and gondolas to load with coal came i by telephone and telegraph like had not happened i at least 10 years. Demand was so joyously high.

The Big War was on – and just like in World War I the U.S. Navy Department chose Pocahontas Coal power its remaining coal-fired ships worldwide, thu greatly benefitting all three Pocahontas Railroads.

In 1938, Princeton Shops had begun building i own 50-ton-capacity hoppers to supplement the b now rebuilt and lowered capacity Class G-3 and G- gondolas. This was good for the employment pictu of Princeton and surrounding area bread winners.

The new cars with the larger letters spellin "VIRGINIAN" on the side sheets – probably the lar est name in the rail industry for many years – wer ll built in a brand-new and large, multi-track black metal building behind the Princeton erecting shop.

This, by the way, is the largest structure still standing on this flat 106-acre plot of land following an aborted attempt to preserve several original shop buildings after the whole area was placed on the National Register of Historical Places about 10 years ago.

But how these shops hummed during the war years. As many as 1,000 men earned good livings during the 1940s at many skills and trades within Princeton Shops. It was the largest employer for several surrounding counties in both West Virginia and Virginia for many decades, coming in over the Mercer Board of Education and the post-war Maidenform Brassiere Company.

Princeton Shops repaired all VGN's classes of steam power and freight cars – plus constructing thousands of new cars of 70 tons capacity mainly during the 1950s. The men also earned a reputation for very good work – from routine maintenance to complete rebuilding or Class 3 steam engine repairs.

Thus, when the good word quickly got around, these mechanics also repaired "foreign road" motive power in both World Wars, such as "U.S."-lettered Mikados and some other locomotives from the Atlantic Coast Line Railroad when that company's shops temporarily could not handle their own work.

In 1947, just after WWII, more coal traffic and the gradual and simple wearing out of some of the 36 individual engine units of the EL-3A jackshaft electric – now all more than 20 years old, Virginian needed more "new" locomotives.

In keeping with management's always and ever frugal ways, a good bargain appeared in the third-hand locomotive market. N&W had sold several of its early homemade Y Class 2-8-8-2s to the Santa Fe at the beginning of World War II to assure that its classiest passenger and freight trains got "over the road" during the Big War.

This meant climbing the three-per-cent-plus grades of Raton Pass and others in the deserts of northeastern New Mexico. So those packed trains like The *Super Chief* and other famous heavily-patronized first-class runs – like the ever-vital "Main"-numbered troop trains – were entrusted to former N&W Mallets for the duration of the conflict.

A rather astounding set of circumstances. But the old Mallets surely got the job done over those grueling grades, rather slowly but reliably. And best of all, for those of us who never could have seen such smoky and spectacular sights, some great, well composed and memorable photographs were taken along this historic line by famed Western railroad photographers like Richard Kindig and his colleagues.

Following wartime service over the Southern Rocky Mountains, Santa Fe soon retired the N&W

GN Class USA 2-8-8-2 No. 711 looking spectacular after her probable last overhaul and gloss locomotive black paint job at Princeton Shops. August 1, 1950. (August A. Thieme, Jr., photo, Lloyd D. Lewis collection)

The day is May 25, 1953, just in front of the Elmore Steam Shop, so called because the rectangular building had neither a roundhouse nor a turntable. Class USD, rebuilt from a class USA Class, Mallet No. 701 is in for servicing between mine runs. (Lloyd D. Lewis collection)

behemoths and set them aside in places like behind the Belen backshops south of Albuquerque. They sat for months, while Santa Fe tried to sell them. And then came a call from Princeton, way back east in the hills from whence the big engines had come in the first place.

So, VGN came to buy seven of the now third-hand engines, had them hauled east via the New York Central at Elkhart, Indiana, and probably picked them up one by one at the DB Tower VGN-NYC interchange near Alloy, east of Charleston, in 1947.

Hauled by local freights to Princeton Shops, the experts there completely rehabilitated the new Nos. 736-742, rewheeled them in the erecting shops, the last major steam work done there – and painted them glossy locomotive black for break-in service.

Company photographer George King Shands – who was the fulltime general foreman of the Narrows Power Plant for many years – followed the 736 westbound on a train of loads from Elmore for Gilbert Yard down the Guyandotte River Branch. He shot several great 4x5 negatives with his press camera, including several for the next VGN company annual report.

This document also showcased a series of four photos of one of the Class USE engines being inspected, worked over and rewheeled in the shops, some of the first photos ever published in these valuable reports, which are now, of course, quite historical.

With the seven third-hand USE Class Mallets performing well on all mine branches west of Elmore, attention was turned once again to the aging but pioneering and revolutionary EL-3As. The jackshafts which once were the public image of the little VGN – were getting older and needed replacement.

Their "cast-iron generation" had come and gone, so VGN turned to General Electric Company's electric locomotives plant in Erie, Pennsylvania, the plant which to this day produces many of the most successful diesel locomotives in the world.

What VGN's and GE's practical engineers and stylish designers came up with was – save for the flashy yellow and black diesel paint scheme a few years later – a real stroke of not only extreme power and efficiency but a "look" that one would never associate with this down-to-earth coal hauler.

Tall and very handsome were the four Class EL-2B semi-permanently coupled giants of the rails. They were assigned road numbers 125-128 and their beautiful bulk soon endeared them to T&E crews and all VGN employees as not only extremely powerful but also a real treat to look at.

Whereas the EL-3As were all long, strong and steel brawn – and were the largest engines in the world in the mid-1920s and for years thereafter (very common to all phases of VGN operations) – the "squareheads" obviously looked like pure mountain locomotives.

On the other hand, the at-once dubbed "streamers," set us all back when we first saw them. Their huge carbodies sure looked a lot like the EMD diesel-electric cab units – and they sure were tall!

This author was quite privileged as a 16-year-old in Elmore Yard just before all electrics quit running in 1962 to climb up the vertical steps to the spacious front cab of an eastbound Roanoke Run. Upon looking at a company diagram shortly afterward, I discovered that I was 15 feet up in the air off the rails. I would have believed 25 feet.

GE really went to work with the publicity on these four very unusual engines and commissioned several versions of what amounted to architect's drawings before they were produced. The Erie folks also took lots of photos both on the East Erie Commercial Railroad test track and in service between Mullens and Roanoke.

Of course, company photographer George Shands photographed them for the 1948 annual report and for a few books of that late 1940's time frame. That simple yet effective paint scheme also turned many an eye toward the tracks as they hummed by, emitting hardly any sounds at all, even on the steepest grades.

Locomotive black covered most of the 150-foot-long gargantuan double units but the long yellow striping and that large VGN logo really set off the whole scheme.

PR and puffery aside, the four electrics performed spectacularly. Everyone loved them from top management to the men who ran them every day to employees along the line.

These were no lightweights, tipping the scales at just more than one million pounds – 1,033,832 pounds to be exact. They could produce 6,800 horsepower – and I wonder just how much they could have pulled. Does any reader know of any train length or train weight testing performed using the EL-2Bs? I would sure like to know.

Regenerative braking was a big feature – as on both of the other classes of VGN electrics. That was like getting real bangs for your bucks:

After ascending any grades on line, once the train started down the other side, the electrical system actually put voltage back into the catenary and thus back into the Narrows Power Plant to be used by other trains going up other grades. Pretty darn slick!

Unfortunately, the EL-2Bs only had an existence of 15 years or so and were cut up by a Richmond, Virginia, scrap dealer about 1963 after N&W took all VGN electrics out of service on Saturday evening, June 20, 1962. The only surviving parts were the motor-generator sets which were sold to the U.S. Navy.

Soon after Virginian's acquisition of the seven third-hand 2-8-8-2 ex-N&W and ex-Santa Fe Mallets – and those unforgettable "streamliners," the need for more 0-8-0 switchers came to the fore. The VGN to that point had only five real switchers, the Nos. 1-5 of Class SA built by both American and Baldwin in 1909 and 1910 – the first locomotives designed after VGN was chartered on March 8, 1907.

Of these, No. 4 is the only surviving VGN steamer and currently is on display at the Virginia Museum of Transportation in Roanoke. However, its previous home was in Princeton City Park from May 1957 until August 1968, when it was hauled to Roanoke in

Truly dramatic is this scene of Class USA No. 712 arriving Elmore Yard near the end of steam with a mine run off the Guyandotte River Line or one of its two branches. The head brakeman at left is ready to throw the next switch as the beautiful behemoth "whomps" and chugs slowly forward in this great vertical shot. (Ben F. Cutler Photo, Lloyd D. Lewis collection)

Class USB No. 727 big 2-8-8-2 at Page Engine Terminal with hostler looking at photographer. September 1953. (Lloyd D. Lewis collection)

the consist of Local Freight No. 64 after a short court dispute.

The No. 4 had really been allowed to deteriorate in Princeton, but no one stepped forward to fix her up, as did the former Roanoke Transportation Museum before a formal dedication in May, 1969. Bright and shiny she became, all over again.

To get more switchers at this late date in the Steam Era, motive power folks heard of a really good deal in 1949 available from neighboring C&O. But this time the used engine agreement really was second hand, not third hand as with the USEs.

C&O had ordered about 45 of its new Class C-16 eight-wheel switchers from Lima in 1945 for distribution all over the system. All of sudden, new Chessie Chairman Robert R. Young took over the line in its Cleveland, Ohio, headquarters and things changed very quickly.

Young's plans for modernizing "Chessie's Road" passenger trains worked reasonably well, except for the planned but never operated streamlined "Chessie" passenger service, and the three steam-turbine-electric locomotives, which were scrapped when only three years old.

Also about this time, the Electro-Motive Division of General Motors introduced its General Purpose 1,750-horsepower diesel-electric locomotives – and

C&O bit hard, eventually ordering hundreds of th new model.

Soon, the Class C-16 0-8-0s, only four years olc went on the market. VGN bought 15 in 1950 at bargain price of $25,000 each, classed them SB, an retained their C&O numbers, 240-254. They serve at many points on the railway until the very end c steam, which was only seven years hence. They wer also the last steam locomotives VGN ever bought.

SB No. 251 earned a unique place in VGN Histor becoming the last VGN steamer ever to turn a whee in regular service while serving as Princeton Shoj switcher on the evening of June 1, 1957.

N&W bought C&O's newest C-16s, 30 in all, an classed them S-1. They lasted only about 11 years an also were among the last very few steamers to oper ate on this larger line in the coalfields in the first fe months of early 1960. In the meantime, the Roanok steam experts – who were definitely among the bes in the world in any era – began tinkering with thei nearly-new Lima products. The result of improvin on the S-1s was a splendid brand-new batch of N&W Class S-1as, the last of which – No. 244 – was th last steam locomotive ever to be manufactured in th United States – in 1953 by Roanoke Shops.

Dozens of Fairbanks-Morse diesel-electrics arrive on the VGN soon after VGN officers and the boar of directors came to the inevitable conclusion tha

50

l American railways – except that last holdout, the &W – had already dieselized for a variety of reasons.

Thus, at his boss' direction, VGN Master Mehanic George T. Strong, Jr., of Princeton journeyed arting about 1952 to all diesel builders – and took opious notes.

Strong is the man who recommended to his mangement and the board that Fairbanks-Morse & Comany of Beloit, Wisconsin, be contracted and committed to construct almost the entire Virginian fleet of ew motive in both 1,600 and 2,400-horsepower verons of squared-off carbodies.

And, in keeping with the 50-year VGN traditions, he 25 largest ones – in a model named "Train Mas-er" – were among the largest and most powerful being built on the planet at that time. These 2,400 HP odel H-24-66 units were classified DE-RS on the GN.

But not just any paint scheme would do for these onsters of the rails. With a train of thought like ose who designed the carbodies and paint schemes f the 1948 EL-2Bs, VGN mechanical men came up ith a very striking yellow body with black striping nd red lining all around and about the large white GN logo on both ends of the total of 66 units.

This included the second-hand 44-ton General lectric switcher numbered 6, also the recipient of is outstanding paint scheme.

Their visibility was outstanding at grade crossgs, the only drawback being that not until they were re-lettered for N&W after December 1st, 1959, were their black numerals painted on the sides of their cabs, originally making their exact identification quite difficult from a distance.

The first batch of Virginian Class DE-S 1,600 HP road-switchers, F-M model H-16-44, was numbered 10 through 47, adequate for current and future predicted traffic levels on the Roanoke-to-Sewalls Point Norfolk Division, where most were assigned to both road and yard switching services.

These "little Fairbanks" 1600 HP engines were also used for switching on the West End New River Division in the West Virginia coalfields, for example, in Princeton and Elmore Yards in car classification duties.

Then the unexpected happened when Class DE-S units 23 and 28 tore through a slide in an unprotected cut at Huddleston, Virginia, about 20 miles east of Roanoke in October 1957. The locomotives were soon hauled very dead in tow to Princeton Shops where mechanical men determined after many inspections that they were both total losses.

Thus, the 48 and the 49 were delivered from Beloit and took their places on the roster not long before the N&W took over. Also, the 23 and the 28 became two of the very few Virginian locomotives whose numbers were vacated.

More important, the 48 and the 49 also closed out the history of all purchases of all new and used VGN motive power, save for the EL-C rectifier electrics, which have been dealt with previously in this book.

ass USE No. 737 looking spanking brand new in 1948 outside Princeton Shops after overhaul for further coal train service. She looks great r a third-hand N&W Roanoke product! (Malcolm McCarter collection)

Massive is the only word that comes to mind when gazing at VGN USE No. 740 outside its new home of about one year in August 1949. Elmore Steam Shop is the last place that this and her six sisters will ever call home — and she will be retired and then sent off to the scrap yard in about five or six years. The everlasting hills of Wyoming County, West Virginia, look down on the coal mining activity that has been g[o]-ing on for about 50 years as of the date of this shot. More than 60 years later, the hauling of the black diamonds continues under the fourth railroad name here. (Credit one of the very first active VGN historians, Norfolk newspaperman H. Reid, for this silent study of huge steam power, Lloyd D. Lewis collection)

A study of a very attractive steam locomotive — VGN PA Class Pacific No. 213, one of a class of six built by American Locomotive Works in Richmond, Virginia, in 1920. With 10 new Pullman-built heavyweight coaches and some headend cars, Virginian completely re-equipped its mainline passenger trains. These were the steam engines that pulled "The Cinder Specials" of this author's childhood. The 213 is at the station stop at the Algonquin coal company store, a rare instance where such a building did double duty. It's 1948 and the train is daily westbound first-class "Cinder Special" No. 3. (Ben F. Cutler Photo, Lloyd D. Lewis collection)

New-to-Virginian Railway Class SB 0-8-0 No. 243 builds up a nice head of steam and black smoke and also takes on water at the stand-alone water column on the east bank of the Guyandotte River not long after her purchase from C&O in 1948 as a practically new locomotive. East End Elmore Yard Office is out of the photo to the right. (Malcolm McCarter collection.)

Fairbanks-Morse Train Master (also known as model H-24-66) No. 56 is seen here at Princeton in June, 1959. Diesels of this model were the predominant type used in West Virginia. (R. D. Patton photo, Lloyd D. Lewis collection)

Fairbanks-Morse 1600 HP model H-16-44 No. 31, VGN class DE-S, at Oak Hill, date unknown. While predominantly used east of Roanoke, Va., diesels of this model were also used in W.Va. (Lloyd D. Lewis collection)

5: Passenger Service

The Virginian Railway fulfilled its primary purpose better than most other railways and certainly better than most corporations ever did; that was to haul fine grades of bituminous coal from several counties in southern West Virginia eastbound to one and later two deepwater coal piers at Sewalls Point, Virginia, on the eastern edge of the City of Norfolk on the Port of Hampton Roads.

In later years, coal traffic was also shipped westbound, and four scheduled daily time freights – Nos. 71, 72, 73 and 74 – operated on the mainline from Deepwater to Norfolk. Two more – Nos. 98 and 99 – were run in connection with the Chesapeake & Ohio

both ways on the Guyandotte River Line during th[e] 1930s.

Virginian's original goal was certainly not to pro[vide] passenger service of any class to its customer[s] and on-line citizens. However, in the first two decade[s] of VGN's existence – 1910-1930 – this service wa[s] certainly both a convenience and a necessity – mainl[y] because virtually no county roads or state highway[s] existed at all in the railway's Mountain State terri[tory].

As noted elsewhere in this book, coal mine branch[es] built after 1930 did not offer passenger train ser[vice]

Famous railway photographer Richard J. Cook of the Cleveland, Ohio, area certainly earned his reputation this day as he climbed up and up off West Virginia State Route No. 10 to get to the Virginian grade on one of the steepest sections of Clarks Gap Mountain Grade at least 10C [100] feet above the Garwood coal camp. And what a fine photo he took here! Westbound No. 3 – or "The Cinder Special" to lots of us close to the scene — drifts down "The Hill" behind PA Class Pacific No. 213 and its usual three-car consist over the spectacular double-track bridge with the highest Cooper weight rating. We can even see a few passengers in the second coach and Railway Post Office car No. 150 has its door open to take advantage of the cool breezes of June 14, 1950 — at (as was Cook's good habit) exactly 11:56 a.m. Seems to be no reason today to be anything but "on the advertised". (Richard J. Cook photo, Lloyd D. Lewis collection)

ice because the level of road construction had, by that time, achieved an acceptable level for residents to rive their own vehicles across the hills and through he valleys of this region.

From its earliest days of construction, local folks ooked to the Deepwater Railway in West Virginia – nd its counterpart Tidewater Railway in the state of Virginia – to let them ride its early way freights and o doubt even its construction trains. Anything was etter than walking, riding the Old Gray Mare and orse- and mule-drawn buggies and buckboards – to nywhere and back.

No doubt some passenger transportation was al- owed on the Deepwater and Tidewater lines even in- ormally before tickets were printed and the service vas thus free at the conductor's discretion. However, his was made a matter of company policy with the ublication on Sunday, June 30, 1907, of VGN's Time 'able No. 1 of its originally-named Deepwater Divi- ion from Deepwater to Matoaka, West Virginia.

No. 6 of the six instructions issued by Superinten- ent O. B. Johnson read "Passengers will be carried n all way freight trains." That meant in standard vooden cupola cabooses, of which VGN eventually ostered nearly 100.

"Way freights" were also later defined in public imetables as "local freights," of which VGN had at east one pair on each subdivision. But, they never arried passengers at any time in their years of ser- ice.

By the time the railway's probable first through imetable dated April, 1909, was printed in *The Of- icial Guide of the Railways*, President Henry Hud- leston Rogers' company offered dependable but slow aily passenger train service all the way from Norfolk o Deepwater.

After Virginian's through service had been estab- shed for a few decades, to travel from one end of the ine to another took two days – with the usual stop- ver in Roanoke for one night. This, of course, com- ared quite unfavorably with N&W and C&O service n one day only.

However, VGN's management obviously kept the tatus quo in order to keep its first-class trains from iterally getting in the way of all that coal, which re- lly was first class.

In fact, the earliest timetables show the 435-mile- ong, two-state journey requiring three days! First,

3-103	Mls.	*August 14, 1949.*	104-4
		LEAVE] [ARRIVE	
*7 30 A M	243.1	+...... Roanoke	4 35 P M
f7 43 "	250.9	+........Salem.........	f4 20 "
f8 03 "	262.0	.......LaFayette....Δ	f3 59 "
f8 11 "	266.3	...... Ironto ....Δ	f3 51 "
f8 21 "	272.4	+......Ellett........Δ	f3 41 "
f8 32 "	278.3	.....Merrimac ....Δ	f3 29 "
8 44 "	284.2	........Pepper........□	3 17 "
8 52 "	287.7	+...Whitethorne......	3 08 "
f9 10 "	296.0	...Goodwin's Ferry..Δ	f2 47 "
f9 14 "	298.2	.....Eggleston....Δ	f2 47 "
f9 24 "	303.4	+ { Pembroke } .. { *Mountain Lake* }	f2 37 "
f9 34 "	309.2	........Norcross.....Δ	f2 26 "
f9 43 "	314.1	.Celco (North Pearisburg).□	f2 16 "
f9 50 "	317.4	+..... Narrows	f2 09 "
f9 58 "	320.8	+..... Rich Creek	f2 01 "
f10 12 "	327.8	...Kellysville, W.Va..Δ	f1 44 "
f10 17 "	329.8	......Oakvale.....Δ	f1 40 "
10 53 "	340.2	+.....Princeton......	1 18 "
f11 03 "	345.0	.......Kegley......Δ	f1 03 "
11 30 "	356.2	+......Matoaka	12 38 "
11 42 "	361.3	+.......Algonquin	12 27 "
f11 58 A M	367.8	+.......Herndon......Δ	f12 10 "
12 03 P M	371.1	..........Bud.........Δ	12 01 P M
f12 11 "	372.0	........Alpoca ....Δ	f11 56 A M
12 21 "	374.7	......Eimore........Δ	11 48 "
f12 36 "	376.7	+......Mullens ......Δ	f11 40 "
f12 52 "	381.7	+......Maben........Δ	f11 15 "
f1 00 "	385.6	.......Hotchkiss.......Δ	f11 07 "
f1 06 "	387.9	+......Slab Fork.......Δ	f11 02 "
f1 16 "	392.2	+.......Lester ....Δ	f10 52 "
1 22 "	394.6	........Surveyor.......Δ	10 46 "
1 34 "	398.6	........Eccles ....Δ	10 37 "
f1 40 "	400.6	+........ Harper.......Δ	f10 32 "
f1 52 "	406.4	........Cirtsville......Δ	f10 18 "
f1 59 "	409.1	+.........Pax..........Δ	f10 12 "
f2 01 "	409.9	....Long Branch.....Δ	f10 10 "
f2 05 "	411.6	.......Lively........Δ	f10 07 "
f2 13 "	414.8	........Dothan........Δ	f10 00 "
f2 21 "	417.7	....Oak Hill Junc...Δ	f9 52 "
f2 29 "	421.1	........Wriston......Δ	f9 42 "
2 46 "	426.8	+........Page........Δ	9 28 "
f2 59 "	430.3	..Beards Junction .Δ	f9 14 "
3 14 "	434.6	..West Deepwater .Δ	9 03 "
3 20 "	435.0	.....D. B. Tower......	9 00 "
g3 22 "	435.3	......Alloy.........	g8 56 "
g3 24 "	436.6	......Boomer.......	g8 54 "
g3 27 "	438.2	.......Longacre......	g8 50 "
g3 29 "	439.0	.......Smithers.....	g8 47 "
g3 31 "	439.8	...{ Cannelton }...{ (Montgomery) }	g8 45 "
g3 38 "	442.8	........London........	g8 37 "
g3 45 "	447.0	......Glasgow.......	g8 31 "
g3 47 "	447.8	.....Cedar Grove.....	g8 28 "
g3 57 "	452.3	.......Dickinson......	g8 18 "
g4 00 "	454.1	.......Witcher......	g8 15 "
g4 02 "	455.5	........Belle	g8 13 "
g4 05 "	458.8	........Levi........	g8 10 "
g4 07 "	460.4	........Malden......	g8 08 "
*4 25 P M	466.1	+Charleston (N.Y.C. Sta.)..	*7 55 A M
....	.....	ARRIVE] [LEAVE	....

1949 public timetable for VGN passenger trains that operated in West Virginia. Note that the trains operated via New York Central from DB Tower to Charleston.

there was the always and forever stopover from both directions in Roanoke. In addition, the public sched- ule of February 2, 1909, shows a trip of 10 hours and 10 minutes westbound for 97 miles on Train No. 1 from Roanoke to Princeton, stopping for the night at 5:40 p.m.

Preparations for this service involved the hiring and training of depot ticket agents and the printing of public timetable schedules and tickets, plus the outfitting of waiting rooms of several sizes. These ranged from the large Norfolk Terminal Station to the road's moderate capacity station at Roanoke, the road's only original brick station, and the many smaller stations. And, all stations in Virginia had to be equipped with two race-segregated waiting rooms.

Three classes of varnished wooden, coaches were bought, for a total of 20 cars. To pull them, six American Standard or Eight Wheel 4-4-0 steam locomotives numbered 100-105 and classed EA, and four Ten-Wheeler type 4-6-0s numbered 200-203 and classed TA, were purchased from American Locomotive Company's Richmond Works.

In fact, the four TAs arrived so early that neither their coaches nor the lines on which they were to run were complete. So, VGN leased them for several months to arch rival Norfolk & Western for Pocahontas Division first-class service in West Virginia.

Standard uniforms were worn by conductors and trainmen, and special pages of instructions were printed in the employees' timetables.

As on most railways, dispatchers were supposed to give these "first class" passenger trains priority over all other trains. That was true on VGN competitors N&W and C&O. However, on VGN, things just did not work out that way, as VGN author H. Reid in his 1961 Kalmbach book *The Virginian Railway* wrote in his own brief and partially quoted poem at the end:

"Three and Four went in the hole
To let the drags by toting coal"

Within the Mountain State, that first throug public timetable provided for Train Nos. 1 and 2 fror Deepwater through Maben, Mullens and Matoak to Princeton, with the last station in West Virgini named "East River Yard," which was soon change to Kellysville. These trains, of course, also ran fror there through Rich Creek, Roanoke, Victoria and int Norfolk every day of the week.

No. 1 departed Princeton at 11 a.m. each day an arrived Deepwater for its scheduled connection wit the C&O at 3:45 p.m. That's four hours and 45 min utes to travel 95 miles – a veritable stock car race i 1909 compared with what local folks were used to.

No. 2 departed its C&O connection at Deepwate at 5:45 a.m. each day and arrived Princeton at 10:3 a.m., which is exactly the same timing.

In addition, two pair of passenger trains ran onl from Page to Deepwater – as a probable holdover fror Deepwater Railway days. These 8.2 miles – especia ly alongside the four miles down the steep banks c Loup Creek from the Robson sawmill to Deepwater were isolated except for the single rail line.

A few local men who lived along Loup Creek prot ably were still working at this sawmill – the Deepwa ter Railway's first customer – by 1909.

However, many more needed reliable, year-roun transportation to the first coal mine on the propert This was the Rogers-owned Loup Creek Coal & Col Company up a hollow to the east of Page Steam Sho which lasted many years.

Princeton was Virginian's princip shop town, located on the main line just before it passed into Virginia. The large passenger station and office building is seen in this August 1954 photo with No. 3, leaving, after doing some business, with its usual light Pacific locomotive and three cars. (Jay Williams collection)

These two pair of short trains operated as follows, all on 30-minute schedules for the 8.4-mile trip, which paralleled no roads from Robson down the creek – and there are still roads near this line today, more than 100 years later:

No. 3 operated daily except Monday, leaving Page at 4:45 p.m., arriving Deepwater via Robson at 5:15 a.m.

No. 4 daily except Sunday, leaving Deepwater at 6 a.m., arriving Page at 6:30 a.m.

No. 5 Monday only, leaving Page at 4:30 p.m. and arriving Deepwater at 5 a.m.

No. 6 Sunday only, leaving Deepwater at 4:15 a.m., arriving Page at 4:45 a.m.

In the early 1910s, Virginian's small Passenger Department got a bit fancy, publishing public timetables for several years with a bright orange cover, which the VGN termed "Virginian Orange." This color was reportedly chosen by long-time General Manager Henning Fernstrom, whose earlier career had been with the Milwaukee Road out west, which had used this shade extensively for years.

The cover depicted an engaging scene: an orange sky over a long VGN passenger train alongside what appears to be New River in Western Virginia.

Also about this time, VGN started painting its all new station buildings and outhouses, section houses, etc., and wooden coaches in this same attractive shade of orange.

Apparently no freight service equipment – or any locomotives at all – were painted orange, which certainly would have been a strange sight to see.

Competitor C&O also painted its own depots and some of its coaches virtually the same color until 1923, but this unusual yet attractive scheme was gradually

Above: Three-car Train No. 4 behind PA Class Pacific No. 211 at Princeton depot on its way from Charleston to Roanoke. January or February 1942. (E. W. Anderson Photo, collection of Charles Arnold)

Below: This is Train No. 3, also pausing at the passenger depot in the author's hometown of Princeton, West Virginia, about 1955. This was probably shortly before the last run from Page to Hales Gap, West Virginia, and back on July 11 that year. (Jay Williams collection)

replaced by gray with dark red trim on VGN sometime before World War II.

The one Virginian station that kept its orange colors, probably because of its remoteness in those early days, until it was demolished after the VGN-N&W

1959 merger, was tiny Phenix, Virginia, between Roanoke and Victoria, on the Third Subdivision.

Incidentally, the line's first and long-time General Passenger Agent was named S. M. Adsit, and was one of a small group of veteran and probably career Virginian manager/employees whose last names were chosen to paint onto signs and hang on station buildings in the very early times.

These villages – such as Adsit, Virginia – were generally in remote areas where, presumably, the company needed to establish an operational point, for example, a water tank and/or a coal dock for replenishing of steam locomotives. And even though there is no service in Adsit today, the village name remains on the highway maps.

As soon as the entire 435-mile-long VGN mainline was completed in early January, 1909, engineering forces were sent out to survey, plot and plumb bob branch lines that made more and even more coal mine sites accessible to rail transportation. (Please see Chapter 2 for histories of all branch lines and spurs.)

Virtually all except the shortest of branches had odd- and even-numbered mixed freight and passenger train service established as soon as coal was available for mining and hauling. In these cases, one crew and set of passenger equipment ran up several branch line hollows in one day and used many different many train numbers.

This practice was long before established by both N&W and C&O in this region. For example, C&O had a series of train numbers with the engaging nickname of "Fanny" with a mainline connection at the busy Prince station very deep in New River Gorge.

Roads and even horse and foot trails were quite scarce in this area before C&O arrived in the early 1870s to develop and otherwise industrialize these areas to an almost unbelievable extent – the way that VGN and N&W also accomplished in their respective coalfields.

This writer recalls seeing at least once in the mid 1950s alongside the VGN mainline east of Matoaka in Mercer County the N&W's own version of this convenience for passengers in those still pre-decent highway and road days.

This train ran every day out of Bluefield, West Virginia, and covered about 18 separate and short train schedules on the complex Bluestone Branch, leaving the mainline at Bluestone Junction about eight miles west of both Bluefields (Va. and W.Va.) The usual consist was an N&W E-2a Pacific, a baggage car and perhaps two heavy weight coaches of the 1600 series. (The Bluestone Branch is still on the ground except for the Turkey Gap and perhaps other short trackage. This is certainly in keeping with the usual N&W practice of not tearing up the abandoned right-of-way because the Coal Department and the coal operators believe there is still plenty of mineable and haulable coal in those ridges.)

This 1930s photo shows the Mullens depot area with Train No. 14 at left (operating from Princeton up the Stone Coal and Winding Gulf Branches) and mainline local No. 3 at right with a Virginian business or parlor car on the rear. (TLC collection)

This is a practically ancient, very rare action shot of a VGN local accommodation passenger train — possibly No. 5 or No. 6 — but not No. 3 or No. 4. It is quite hard to determine location, except west of Mullens. Note this TA 4-6-0 locomotive is possibly in Fayette County, near Lively or Lax, circa 1920. (Lloyd D. Lewis collection)

Neither VGN's mileage nor its number of branch lines were as many as its neighbors, but its own short coalfield trains had the same purposes: to feed passengers, express and the U.S. Mail – and sometimes box car freight – to mainline trains.

And these "plug runs" were certainly the most desirable for the train and engine service crews, who were assigned to them by their respective dates of seniority with the railway company. These men were home every night and did not have to complain about lays on the road under terrible weather and other operating conditions.

This was accomplished in a big way at Mullens where the Winding Gulf Branch entered the mainline and also where the "main stem" branch passenger runs met the real mainline passenger trains.

One example of a true mixed train of both wooden coaches and freight cars, other than coal hoppers and gondolas, was up the Virginian & Western Branch running steeply upgrade out of Maben and Virwest, Wyoming County, just five miles west of Mullens.

In many instances, these branch line crews made several roundtrips over these individual branch lines beginning early each morning and ending about time for coal miners to get off their first shifts and get home – or about 5 p.m.

This all predictably came to an end in the mid-1930s. By this time the railway – and C&O and N&W – could show the West Virginia Public Service Commission that its losses for operating every day were quite large percentages above the meager revenue brought in by those numerous residents who did not have a car – or even a faithful mare.

Many who rode the trains were VGN employees traveling from or back to home terminals at Elmore or other coal towns to catch and operate mine runs. They rode these two-to-three–car trains for free when they produced the latest annual pass and presented it to the conductor.

Virginian's last New River Division daily passenger train ran on July 11, 1955.

Nowhere did Virginian host an honest-to-Pete, genuine public "name train," unlike both N&W and C&O and their fleets of spectacular and modern daily train services. VGN's "first-class trains" were designated strictly by numbers only – except for the very affectionate nickname given all this railway's passenger runs – and no doubt hundreds and maybe thousands of others throughout the U.S.

They were our own treasured "Cinder Specials," which "honored" the fact that nowhere in West Virginia did VGN ever operate an air-conditioned passenger service except for the private cars that made up the annual system-wide executive inspection runs and other special and very rare trains.

A prime example of this was the *Rexall Special* that ran eastbound only at night over VGN from Deepwater to Roanoke in the late 1930s. This dru[m] company's train was headed by a VGN class MC 2-8-[ ] followed by a New York Central 4-8-2 Mohawk!

However, air conditioning or not, we employee[s] and immediate dependent families rode for abs[o]lutely nothing. Plus, as extra free benefits, we als[o] could hear quite clearly the chugging VGN Pacific u[p] front – and sample the "cinder culture" inside for o[ur] entire trip simply by propping up the heavy narro[w] windows inside the 200-series heavyweight coache[s]. So how could we complain?

Train No. 4 heads eastbound, beginning her daily run on August 23, 1953, between Page and Kincaid. PA Class Pacific No. 211 heads up this "Cinder Special" which has two heavyweight 200-series coaches in front of the RPO-baggage car. (Joseph G. Collias Photo, Lloyd D. Lewis collection)

The three car No. 103 is speeding along the New York Central track east of Charleston in this 1944 photo with its usual Pacific type locomotive and three cars, even in the wartime year of 1944. (Glen[n] Grabill Jr. photo, H.H. Harwood, Jr. collection)

Although the Virginian came only within 30 miles of West Virginia's capital, it reached there through trackage rights over New York Central, and its passenger trains served the city. Here one is standing at the Charleston station while an NYC train sits to the right. (Thornton Wise Photo, TLC collection)

Glen Lyn to Princeton

The massive bridge across the New River at Glen Lyn, Va. is widely regarded as the beginning of the VGN in W.Va., even though, strictly speaking, the actual state line is a few hundred yards west of the bridge's west end. Here, three-unit "Squarehead" No. 103 eases across the New River, heading thrice-weekly Princeton-to-Roanoke Local Freight No. 64. As recorded by Photographer Cook, this memorable event occurred at 9:15 a.m., September 4, 1953, and was probably the next train across after that beauty in the photo on the next page. Appalachian Power Company's Glen Lyn coal-burning power plant – a steady VGN customer since 1934 – is somewhat visible at the far left and the U.S. 219-460 bridge is beyond the VGN span. This is the main highway bridge involved in the four-lane project that forced the demolition – except for those still-there piers! – in 1968. (Richard J. Cook photo, TLC collection)

An EL-2B has charge of Manifest Train No. 71, westbound at the west end of the Glen Lyn bridge, ca. 1948. (George K. Shands photo, Lloyd D. Lewis collection)

A westbound train of empty giant VGN gondolas crosses New River at 8:30 a.m., September 4. 1953, behind an EL-2B. This is the bridge about which H. Reid quoted a poetic soul from a long time ago, who described trains which cross this span as "for a few minutes they were like birds." How true, how true! (Richard J. Cook photo, TLC collection)

On June 12, 1956, at 6 p.m., one of the four gorgeous EL-2B "Streamliners" makes a rare solo move across this span – and I reckon we will never know why at this late date. (Richard J. Cook photo, TLC collection)

VGN Extra East No. 108 moves away from the photographer eastbound at the west end of New River Bridge at Glen Lyn, Virginia. This occurred, according to Richard Cook's copious notes, at 5:30 p.m., June 12, 1956. N&W's double track mainline is just out of sight at lower left. (Richard J. Cook photo, TLC collection)

Eastbound Time Freight No. 71 crosses the Virginia-West Virginia state line atop East River Bridge about one-half mile west of Glen Lyn, station. No certain date but about 1950 with a nearly new Class EL-2B electric. (Ben. F. Cutler Photo, Lloyd D. Lewis collection)

Westbound train of empty coal hoppers crosses East River Bridge just west of Glen Lyn. The photographer wrote that the locomotive was either EL-2B No. 125 or 128. July 13, 1948. (Charles A. Brown photo, Lloyd D. Lewis collection)

...stbound electric No. 101 is taking a long train of loads ...ward Sewalls Point, passing one of the streamlined ...-2B electrics that Virginian acquired in 1948 to supple-...ent the old Jack-Shafts, at Kellysville, W. Va. at 4:25 ...m., June 10, 1949. (Richard J. Cook photo, TLC collec-...n)

...ere a set of the famous "Jack-Shaft" electrics, No. 105, ...kes a westbound over one of the trestles near Oakvale, ...est Virginia, on June 13, 1956. (Richard J. Cook Photo, ...C collection)

...mpties roll up Oakvale Mountain toward Princ-...on behind EL-3A No. 100 on the bridge over ...S. 219-460 just east of Oakvale station. Two ...its only. Perhaps 1948. (Ben F. Cutler photo, ...oyd D. Lewis collection)

Class EL-3A No. 101 and a steel caboose pass the unknown photographer at the east end of Princeton Yard on a westbound that could have involved the No. 101 pushing an eastbound coal drag up to Oney Gap Tunnel; an extraordinary move. No certain date. (Jeffry L. Sanders collection)

Eastbound loads behind EL-3A No. 100 pass east end of Princeton Yard with the depot buildings and Princeton Shops in far left background. Mid-1950s. (Jeffry L. Sanders collection)

New Class EL-2B "Streamliner" and westbound train passes the New River Division Headquarters and Passenger Station. The photographer's perch on the Thorn Street Bridge in Princeton gives us a good view of the top of the locomotive. Probably summer 1948. (Ben F. Cutler photo, Lloyd D. Lewis collection)

"Cinder Special" VGN Train No. 3 led by Class PA Pacific No. 215 and just about to pull out of Princeton Depot with a Railway Post Office car and two heavyweight 200-series coaches. This negative probably exposed in 1954 or before the last run on July 11, 1955. (Roy W. Carlson photo, Lloyd D. Lewis collection)

Princeton First Trick dispatcher Arthur Perry wore a tie to work this day in 1956 when he knew George King Shands would be driving 30 miles west from Narrows Power Plant on that day to "shoot" his photo at his proper place in front of the World War II era Centralized Traffic Control board. The board was in its new location about two years in the concrete extension on the second floor of the Princeton Depot after it was moved there from a small brick building just east of the Mullens Depot. (VGN Ry photo, Lloyd D. Lewis collection)

Westbound "Cinder Special," formally VGN first-class Train No. 3, makes its station stop at Princeton in the winter of 1954-55. Standard consist on this dark late morning is Class PA Pacific, RPO/baggage car, and two heavyweight coaches in the 200 series. At left is a wooden caboose, possibly the rear of Local Freight No. 64, here at the end of Mercer Street. (Hardy Trolander Photo, Lloyd D. Lewis collection)

One-sixth of the total of VGN Class EL-3A 36 individual electric locomotive units sit in the dead line east of Princeton Shops and west of the road's turntable and roundhouse there. No. 110 is at the right with virtually new DE-S No. 15 at left. No certain date. (Photo by Ben Perry, Jeff Sanders collection.)

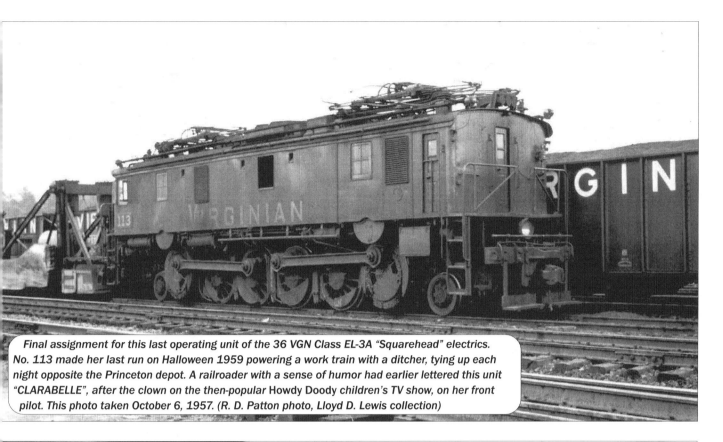

Final assignment for this last operating unit of the 36 VGN Class EL-3A "Squarehead" electrics. No. 113 made her last run on Halloween 1959 powering a work train with a ditcher, tying up each night opposite the Princeton depot. A railroader with a sense of humor had earlier lettered this unit "CLARABELLE", after the clown on the then-popular Howdy Doody children's TV show, on her front pilot. This photo taken October 6, 1957. (R. D. Patton photo, Lloyd D. Lewis collection)

The Virginian station at Princeton stood for many years but was eventually demolished. Today the depot has been rebuilt using original plans, but just not to the same exact size, and it houses a new railroad museum devoted to the Virginian. In this July 29, 1953 scene an MB class 2-8-2 is switching the yard, which is loaded with hopper cars that Virginian lettered so boldly. (H. Reid Photo, TLC collection)

The VGN's only backshop was built at Princeton beginning in 1905. This photo shows, left to right, the car shop (large black structure), coach shop (smaller brick building in front of the car shop), erecting shop (long building under the twin stacks), and machine shop (at right). The yard is behind and the main line loops through the lower right foreground. A transfer table connected the erecting and machine shops. Once employing more than 800 men, the shops only employed about 35 when closed by Norfolk Southern in 1991. (Lloyd D. Lewis collection)

Here a worker turns a driving wheel center on a 90-inch wheel lathe. (Lloyd D. Lewis collection)

An employee is burnishing an engine truck journal on a 90 inch wheel lathe. (Lloyd D. Lewis collection)

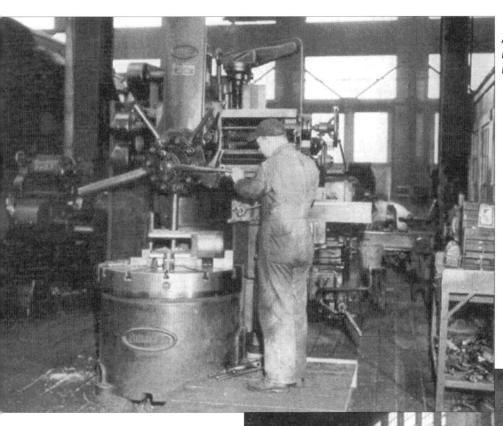

A wrist pin hole being bored in a loco-motive cross-head on a vertical turret lathe. (Lloyd D. Lewis collection)

Steam locomotive driving box equalizer being forged from steel billet on a 3,000 pounds-per-square-inch high frame steam hammer. Probably the largest machine for repairing steam engines. (Lloyd D. Lewis collection)

Newly-renumbered ex-N&W and ex-AT&SF 2-8-8-2 VGN Class USE No. 737 undergoing Class III rehabilitation and rebuilding in the large Erecting Shop at Princeton Shops. At this point the big engine is still missing its wheels and front cylinders. (George King Shands photos from the 1948 Virginian Railway Annual Report, Lloyd D. Lewis collection)

No. 737 now has its wheels and front cylinders. It appears that its Class III rehabilitation and rebuilding is almost complete. (George King Shands photo from the 1948 Virginian Railway Annual Report, Lloyd D. Lewis collection)

Still lettered Virginian, but with post-merger N&W numbers 227-228, this EL-2B has an eastbound coal train at Princeton Yard. The Princeton Shops in the background were VGN's primary shop for steam and diesel work, while electric locomotive work, and some work on diesels, was concentrated at the Mullens Motor Barn. (N&W Railway photo, Lloyd D. Lewis collection)

Princeton to Elmore

Above and Right: One of the four beautiful and stylish EL-2B "Streamliners" hauls an eastbound coal drag with a few cars of valuable time freight as its head cars that could not wait on the next day's No. 72. This train is running pretty fast (note speed blur) crossing the trestle over N&W's Bluestone Branch around the curve from the depot at Matoaka, Mercer County. Matoaka (Indian name for Pocahontas) is visible in the background and was Deepwater Railway's original terminal. In the next four years, VGN Builder Henry Huddleston Rogers – with nearly all his own $40 million – expanded his Deepwater line about 350 miles further east to Sewalls Point – of course for his own profit but also to spite both the N&W and C&O!. (Ben F. Cutler photo, Lloyd D. Lewis collection)

A GE publicity photo of EL-2B No. 125 in snow on the mountain near Clarks Gap. (Lloyd D. Lewis collection)

Opposite and Right: Three more in Cutler's rewarding sequence of EL-2B "Streamliner" No. 128 at the top of Clarks Gap or Algonquin Summit Siding (see also p. 73). At lower left, the proud engineman stands in the doorway, which is nearly 15 feet above the rail. And, at right, the photographer is very lucky to be invited inside the locomotive cab as this author also once experienced. What a genuine natural high! (All three are Ben. F. Cutler photos, Lloyd D. Lewis collection)

Emerging from the tunnel through Clarks Gap at Algonquin in September, 1948, EL-3A No. 104 carries the white flags of an extra. These machines made a steam locomotive-like clanking noise with their side rods as they churned their drivers along, not always quite in unison. The top mounted and polished bell and trimmed windows give a little decoration to the front of these otherwise quite utilitarian locomotives. The catenary pole at the right is the 952nd pole west of the Narrows Power Plant, and is on the north side of the track. (Ben F. Cutler photo, Lloyd D. Lewis collection)

On Garwood Bridge – the last of several spans visible from West Virginia Route No. 10 as VGN climbed Clarks Gap – an unknown "Streamlin er" hauls a VGN Fairbanks-Morse Train Master diesel-electric unit and an eastbound coal drag. The diesel may be on its way from daily duties as Elmore yard switcher – or any mine run – for heavy work at Princeton Shops. Thirty-day inspections of F-Ms and electrics were handled at the Mullens Motor Barn. (Dr. Arthur M. Haelig photo, Lloyd D. Lewis collection)

Covel, West Virginia, with its long curving trestle was always a favorite of Virginian photographers, and here No. 107 has an extra east Hill Run of 28 loads at 10:23 a.m., June 14, 1950. In the town below workers apply a tar-paper roof to one of the houses. (Richard J. Cook Photo, TLC collection)

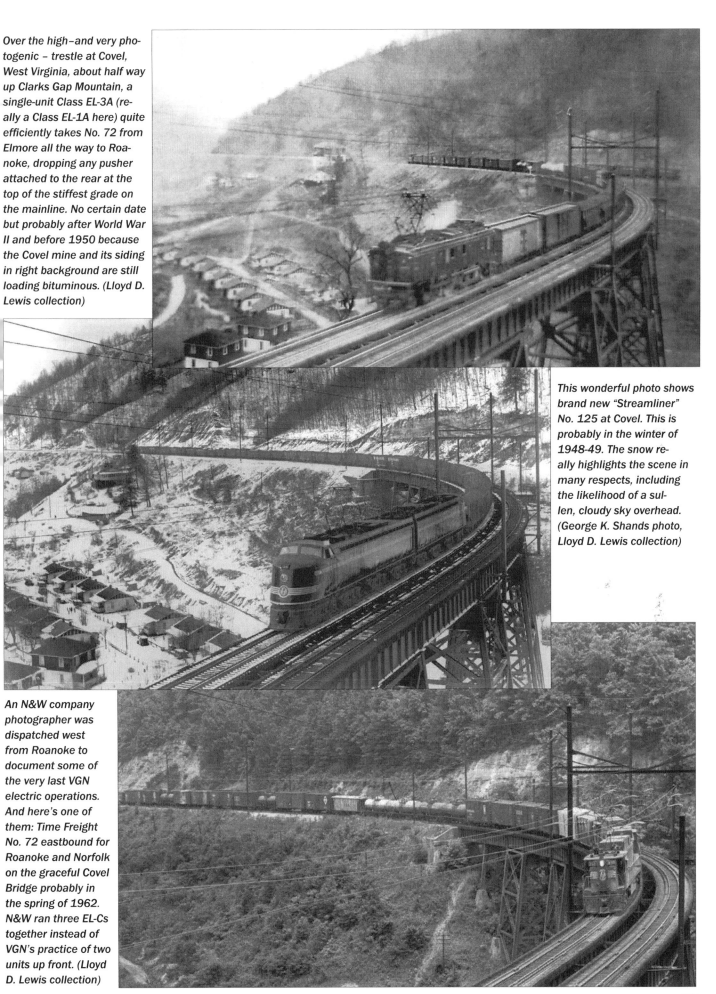

Over the high–and very pho-togenic – trestle at Covel, West Virginia, about half way up Clarks Gap Mountain, a single-unit Class EL-3A (re-ally a Class EL-1A here) quite efficiently takes No. 72 from Elmore all the way to Roa-noke, dropping any pusher attached to the rear at the top of the stiffest grade on the mainline. No certain date but probably after World War II and before 1950 because the Covel mine and its siding in right background are still loading bituminous. (Lloyd D. Lewis collection)

This wonderful photo shows brand new "Streamliner" No. 125 at Covel. This is probably in the winter of 1948-49. The snow re-ally highlights the scene in many respects, including the likelihood of a sul-len, cloudy sky overhead. (George K. Shands photo, Lloyd D. Lewis collection)

An N&W company photographer was dispatched west from Roanoke to document some of the very last VGN electric operations. And here's one of them: Time Freight No. 72 eastbound for Roanoke and Norfolk on the graceful Covel Bridge probably in the spring of 1962. N&W ran three EL-Cs together instead of VGN's practice of two units up front. (Lloyd D. Lewis collection)

Here's a truly dramatic shot of VGN Class MC No. 468 heading up a bullet-nosed N&W streamlined J Class 4-8-4. The fascinating occasion here on Covel Bridge is the detouring of No. 4, the eastbound *Pocahontas* due to a derailment on that road's mainline in McDowell County, as N&W style comes to "VGN blue collar coal culture." And the quite large name on Covel bridge span really stands out! The date is about 1950 and three Rail Photo Service photographers were just plain dead lucky to see it all, at least from Elmore Yard to Garwood – because they then probably got lost in the woods with which they were no doubt so unfamiliar. (Ben F. Cutler photo, Lloyd D. Lewis collection)

Two of the new EL-C electrics have charge of the second of three eastbound Hill Runs operated – this one on October 25, 1956, at approximately 4 p.m. – as one of the initial tests for both VGN and General Electric men to see exactly what they had bought and manufactured. The train had 38 loads and 0 empties for a total of 2,964 tons of revenue on the train. The GE company photographer from Erie, Pennsylvania, was even on hand at Covel with his fancy camera equipment. (General Electric photo, Lloyd D. Lewis collection)

Nearing the end of their too-short careers and the end of VGN's 37½-year-long electrification scheme, an unrelettered N&W EL-2B "Streamliner" pushes the rear of a 3,000-ton Hill Run with another of the four outstanding double units on the front end. The former Virginian Railway steel caboose is safely tucked behind the pusher on Covel bridge as the train bears down on one of the toughest parts of the two-track mainline headed for Clarks Gap Tunnel. November 27, 1961. (Lloyd D. Lewis photo)

Here is busy tipple on the main line at Herndon, with the electrified main line in the foreground. No certain date. (VGN Railway photo, Lloyd D. Lewis collection)

The now long-leveled tipple at Tierney, just west of Herndon, about half way up Clarks Gap Mountain, is seen in 1953. There is a variety of Virginian hopper cars here, including some wooden composite cars and some cars just recently painted. (Pat Dobbin photo, Lloyd D. Lewis collection)

VGN's first historian, H. Reid, was still in his youth in August 1950 as he stood on top of a short cut on the east side of the "Upper Bud Bridge" when he shot EL-3A No. 110 on either a Hill Run or a Roanoke Run. This photo was published in "The Ultimate Aitch's" – his nickname for himself – quite memorable 1961 Kalmbach book titled The Virginian Railway, a tome he worked on for many years while a newspaper reporter. (H. Reid photo, Lloyd D. Lewis collection)

About 1949, westbound "Cinder Special" Train No. 3 crosses the snow-covered landscape, West Virginia State Route 10 and the now long-gone Mullens Drive-In Theatre (at the right edge of the photo). A modern middle school now occupies this former theatre property. (Hardy Trolander photo, Lloyd D. Lewis collection)

A traditional three-unit "Squarehead", whose number we don't know because of the distance, crosses eastbound over yet another of those common large "VIRGINIAN" names lettered in very good white paint. This is what some of us know as the "Upper Bud Bridge" that gives us a view of the Mullens Drive-In Theatre projection booth. The date is March 1950. (Charles A. Brown photo, Lloyd D. Lewis collection)

Ben F. Cutler again shows his sensitivity for railroad photography when he captured this Hill Run or Roanoke Run passing above the Bud coal camp. This looks like "Squarehead" No. 105 this day pulling the loaded large gondolas and smaller hoppers all the way to Clarks Gap. (Ben F Cutler photo, Lloyd D. Lewis collection)

One of the first test runs conducted by General Electric and new owner Virginian Railway of the brand-new Class EL-C rectifiers is shown here as photographed by a GE cameraman on October 25, 1956, on the "Lower Bud Bridge" almost silently lugging about 50 loads of coal around a curve on the double-track line to Clarks Gap Summit. Each of the 12 locomotives, numbered 130-141, produced 3,300 horsepower. Rectifier tubes in each unit converted the 25-cycle alternating current to direct current for use in standard diesel-electric traction motors. (General Electric photo, Lloyd D. Lewis collection)

Three-unit "Squarehead" No. 103 lugs about 50 loads of coal through the Alpoca coal camp near the beginning of the toughest part of Clarks Gap Grade. The weather here is sunny in the summer of 1950 but in these coalfields winter can surely bring on quite dreary skies over the winter landscape. (Ben F. Cutler photo, Lloyd D. Lewis collection)

Photographer Cutler apparently has "chased" No. 103 around the Wyoming County hillside to "Lower Bud Bridge" in about the summer of 1950 as the climb grows ever steeper to reach the maximum of 2.07 per cent in just a few miles for a couple short stretches. These bridge catenary poles are still in place in 2011. (Ben F. Cutler photo, Lloyd D. Lewis collection)

A traditional three-unit, jack-shaft squarehead Class EL-3A electric begins the 14-mile climb to Clarks Gap Summit, as shown in an early 1950s annual report. The new Tralee Tipple fills the space in front of the background hillside as the eastbound coal drag passes three tracks of empties for this part of the railway. (George King Shands Photo, Lloyd D. Lewis collection)

This scene is at Deerfield mine, one of the few located east of Mullens. The modern tipple is seen loading different grades of coal on six tracks into 50-ton Virginian hopper cars in 1950. (George Shands photo, Lloyd D. Lewis collection)

Elmore and Mullens

Train Master unit with wooden caboose Class C-1 No. 96 as East End Elmore Yard Switcher in September 1957. (Gene Huddleston photo, Lloyd D. Lewis collection)

VGN DE-RS Train Master as East End Elmore Yard Switcher on the eastbound double track mainline passing what is probably a two-unit EL-C rectifier electric returning light from pushing a Hill Run to Clarks Gap. "END of CTC TERRITORY" sign applies to lead track that runs behind the former Elmore Steam Shop out of sight to left that was non-signaled in those days. Date is 1959. (Gene Huddleston photo, Lloyd D. Lewis collection)

US Class 2-8-8-2 Mallets No. 703 and stable mate No. 725, are outside Elmore Steam Shop in April 1949 awaiting their next service as the engineer of the 703 inspects the work done on his steed since he last ran her. (Railroad Photographs, Lloyd D. Lewis collection)

On June 23, 1950, Class USA Mallet No. 708, seen here at the Elmore Steam Shop, has about five more years of service in the VGN's bituminous coal fields before both the diesel-electrics and the scrapper move in. (H. Reid photo, Lloyd D. Lewis collection)

An excellent overall scene of the big change at East End Elmore Yard when the diesel-electrics arrived in 1954. Both the 51 and the 61 are busy shifting loads, while in the background, from left to right, are the old steam locomotive water storage tank on the hillside, the concrete coal dock and the then-still-standing Elmore Steam Shop, which is not far at this point from abandonment and demolition. (Peg Dobbin photo for Fairbanks-Morse, H.H. Harwood collection)

Unit No. 51 pulling empty hoppers – and one 105-ton-capacity Class G-3 or G-4 gon load along the east bank of the Guyandotte River past the second (of three) East End Elmore Yard office. Note the opposed-piston engine's white smoke from the 51's stack. That REAL West Virginia icon, the swinging bridge, is stronger here than most but was taken out of service when the new yard office was built further east and to the right of this scene about 25 years ago. (Peg Dobbin photo for Fairbanks-Morse, H.H. Harwood collection)

Here is a truly graphic photo taken in the winter of 1954-55 by VGN Yard Clerk O. W. "Pete" Andrews, who also shot the famous image of the new Train Master and its whole train of loads at Loop Junction, which we will see later. Andrews climbed the coal dock to depict probably the saddest view of the end of VGN steam. Only two locomotives are under steam – one at the left and the Mallet on the right – and we also get a very good view of the rectangular Elmore Steam Shop. (O.W. "Pete" Andrews photo, collection of Jimmy Musser.)

MC Class Mikado No. 464 pauses for repairs and servicing at the Elmore Steam Shop in May 1953. The 1912 Baldwin product only has about two more years before she is scrapped way away from her Home In Those West Virginia Hills. (Photo by William Swartz, collection of Malcolm D. McCarter)

It's quite rare to see a photo taken by a railfan of an approaching train from an opposing train. Especially in the hills and hollers of Elmore, West Virginia, on The Virginian Railway. This one was taken on October 31st, 1959, when the few knowledgeable railfans who could get around in those days were hunting the very last of N&W Class Y6 Mallets about 50 and more miles south of here from Bluefield through the Iaeger coalfield terminal to Williamson. This is VGN Hill Run Extra Class EL-C No. 134 with 71 loads, 0 empties and 5,960 tons of revenue waiting for a clear block on a high signal off to the left. The photographer has ridden Extra 126 West all the way as the EL-2B arrives East End Elmore Yard from Roanoke with four loads, 63 empties and 1,597 tons of revenue. (William B. Gwaltney photo, Lloyd D. Lewis collection)

Virginian cabooses abound at Elmore Yard on July 27, 1948. Needed for the many main line and mine shifter runs that operated out of this central coal fields yard, the wooden cars were kept in top condition. As with many wooden cabooses after years of rough service, the cupolas are stabilized by steel rods with turnbuckles. (H. Reid Photo, Lloyd D. Lewis collection)

The "head shack" (brakeman) of the EL-3A No. 102 walks back to the three-unit behemoth of the rails as his engineer in the cab soon heads for either the west end of Elmore Yard at Gulf Junction or Mullens Motor Barn with a wooden VGN caboose attached, concluding another three Hill Runs up to Clarks Gap at Algonquin Station. Please note the large coal dock and the Elmore Steam Shop in the middle and left backgrounds. All visible earth around the railroad is covered with layers of cinders from the huge steamers which call the steam shop home. In the background just right of the coal dock is the office building of the company that operated the first Itmann Mine there before the company built a new tipple in the late 1940s four miles west on the Guyandotte River Line. Date not certain but probably 1940s. (Jay Williams collection)

AD No. 605 at Elmore Steam Shops near the ready track. (Rev. Wm C. Stearns photo, Lloyd D. Lewis collection)

MC No. 479 pushes Virginian wooden Class C-1 Caboose No. 7 on the westbound mainline track between Elmore Steam Shop and Coal Dock. No date certain. (Stephen P. Davidson photo, Lloyd D. Lewis collection)

Members of the two newest of VGN's three classes of electric locomotives meet head to head on adjacent tracks on Elmore Yard in summer 1957 as the crews exchange greetings. An EL-2B "Streamliner" is at left with an EL-C "Rectifier" at right. (Eugene H. Huddleston Photo, Lloyd D. Lewis collection)

VGN Streamliner No. 228 of the distinguished class of EL-2B electrics awaits a highball at the east end of Elmore Yard on April 21, 1961. N&W influence is all over the place. (Richard D. Patton Photo, Lloyd D. Lewis collection)

Here is an unusual photo with the crew boarding a three-unit Class EL-3A No. 101 about to haul what looks to be at least 20 Virginian Railway wooden cabooses eastbound. This was taken at an uncertain but perhaps 1930s date in what looks like Elmore Yard. Certainly an interesting "caboose hop." (William D. Volkmer Photo, Lloyd D. Lewis collection)

Here's the Elmore Classification Yard just east of Mullens. The yard was expanded and its old hump removed about 1950 when Shands took this photograph. The Elmore Steam Shop is seen in the far right background. (George K. Shands, photo, Lloyd D. Lewis collection)

Train No. 3 is arriving at Mullens on June 18, 1949. The Gulf Junction telegraph office is in the left center background, and the Mullens Motor Barn is out of sight on the left of the photo. PA class Pacific No. 215 has the usual three-car train in tow. (Richard J. Cook photo, Lloyd D. Lewis collection)

Train No. 3 with Pacific No. 215 and three cars is departing Mullens on June 18, 1949. The Motor Barn and trainmaster's office are on the left, while three box cars occupy the freight house track adjacent to the passenger station. (Richard J. Cook photo, Lloyd D. Lewis collection)

Class DE-RS Train Masters Nos. 52 and 53 lead an eastbound train past the station platform at Mullens minutes before tying up in Elmore Yard, just to the east, after a run from Page or Dickinson, on the NYC along the Kanawha River, in the mid-1950s. (Jim Shaw photo, Lloyd D. Lewis collection)

A photo by VGN Company photographer George King Shands depicts the Electric Locomotive Shop at Mullens, West Virginia, from the top of Mullens Hill. Howsomever, VGN folks always called this very up-to-date building the "Mullens Motor Barn." (George K. Shands photo, Lloyd D. Lewis collection)

The new generation is here, as evidenced not only by the approximately four-year-old Train Master diesel-electrics parked next to the much older EL-3A electrics. The most obvious new installation to the trained eye is the relatively new fuel tank for the newcomers and the short line of tank cars that are used to deliver diesel fuel. The old home on the hillside was around for many decades, but is finally gone. September 6, 1958, is the date. (Bob's Photo collection)

Two-year-old Train Master No. 67 – Class DE-RS, standing for diesel-Electric Road Switcher, has just received train orders and a clearance card at Gulf Junction in 1956 and is heading westbound for one or more mines with empty VGN hopper cars to trade for loads. It's return to Elmore Yard may be this very evening. These units often ran double-headed, depending on the work required. (Jim Shaw photo, Lloyd D. Lewis collection)

EL-3A No. 108 and other identical electric units are in front of the Motor Barn next to the double sand towers. Downtown Mullens is partially visible at right and many homes and small businesses have gradually taken over the hillsides beyond. During the 10 decades since the Deepwater Railway was first laid through the farmer's fields here, hundreds of very loyal VGN employees and also the next generation have lived their hard-working lives here. No certain date. (Ben F. Cutler photo, Lloyd D. Lewis collection)

It looks like new EL-2B No. 128 got company management in Norfolk to ask George King Shands to temporarily leave his full-time job as General Foreman of the Narrows (Virginia) Power Plant and drive about 60 miles one way over to the Mullens Motor Barn for a portrait session And here she is! It is circa 1949. Everything in this photo is now (2011) gone– except for the dirt in the foreground and the hillside beyond back of downtown Mullens. (George K. Shands photo, Lloyd D. Lewis collection)

Brand new rectifiers No. 140 and 141 are in front of the Mullens Motor Barn on May 5, 1957. (C. K. Marsh photo, Lloyd D. Lewis collection)

VGN EL-2B "Streamliner" No. 126 – one of the most attractive locomotive classes ever manufactured, in this writer's definite opinion – is parked temporarily below the Mullens Motor Barn water tank and is in front of the Barn. The time is about 1950 – and the world has changed so much since then! (Lloyd D. Lewis collection)

Train Master No. 70, EL-1As Nos. 113 and 115 and the newest type on the line, EL-C Rectifier Nos. 136 and 137 "hang out" with other massive road units behind Mullens Motor Barn on September 7, 1958. (John Sullivan photo, Lloyd D. Lewis collection)

Mullens to Deepwater and Charleston

URSA Heavy Mallet Virginian Railway 2-8-8-2 class USB No. 721 totes a heavy coal drag – one of many thousands run though here in the past 105 or so years – eastbound past the siding at Harmco, West Virginia, in August 1950. It's quite hot today, even in these Southern West Virginia hills just about five miles west of Elmore Yard. (H. Reid photo, Lloyd D. Lewis collection)

Westbound out of Mullens, Class USA Mallet No. 711 trundles a train of empties to the ever-waiting mines at the direction of the car distributor on the second floor of the original Princeton depot. Post-War II but no certain date. (Glenn B. Grabill, Jr. photo, Lloyd D. Lewis collection)

Here is where a good chunk of Virginian hauled coal originated. This is Oglebay Norton Coal Company's underground shaft mine at Otsego, just beyond the northern city limits of Mullens – and one of this railway's earliest and most reliable customers. Date of this photo is June 1954, and the tipple was quite old then – but no mine has existed at Otsego for decades now. Perhaps the most interesting story about this photo – and several more to follow herein – is that it was taken by a photographer employed by C&O's Public Relations & Advertising Department in Cleveland, Ohio. Don't know why these photos were taken – a story of sorts? – but aren't we glad this happened? (C&O Railway photo, C&O Historical Society collection, CSPR 10057.E02)

Another official C&O photo here shows Winding Gulf Coal, Inc.'s, West Gulf Mine on VGN mainline about one mile west of Maben, West Virginia. Date of photo is June 1954. Note the two VGN Class 30000-series gondolas awaiting their loads along with a 50-ton capacity hopper car. No mine has existed in this neighborhood for at least 30 years (as of 2011). This location alongside West Virginia State Route No. 54 is about 10 miles west (geographically north) of Mullens. (C&O Railway photo, C&O Historical Society collection, CSPR 10057.E05)

Probably the best of the few Public Relations photographs taken by company photographer George King Shands and his associate Mr. Burgess, from Sewalls Point Coal Docks. Brother King, besides his long-held duties as General Foreman, Narrows Power Plant, possessed impressive photographic skills which VGN top brass drew on for many of its latter day annual reports. This fine photo of brand-new Train Masters 60 and 64 was taken as Princeton dispatcher Arthur Perry stopped Time Freight No. 71 westbound for a few minutes on the Slab Fork trestle bridge. The full-color result was published on both the front and rear of VGN's 1954 annual report to its pleased stockholders. (George King Shands photo, Lloyd D. Lewis collection)

Four years before George Shands took his photo, Richard J. Cook also discovered the bridge over the coal camp at Slab Fork, site of one of the first Virginian-served mines. As the children play and wash hangs in the breeze below the bridge, Pacific No. 213 with the mail/express car and two steel coaches of Train No. 4 roll overhead at 11:03 a.m., June 13, 1950, headed toward Mullens, Princeton, and later in the day, Roanoke. Under the bridge at left loaded hoppers wait on the mine spur for pickup. (Richard J. Cook photo, Lloyd D. Lewis collection)

This aerial view of the above-ground mine buildings at Slab Fork shows one of the first tipples served by Virginian. This site ran out of coal after the N&W merger, and bituminous is now shipped from deeper parts of this mine on the Winding Gulf Branch on the other side of this mountain via the NS. (Virginian Railway 1947 Annual Report photo, Lloyd D. Lewis collection)

Above and Right: These two photos show eastbound Train No. 4 arriving and departing the tiny station, barely a shelter, at Surveyor, sometime in 1953. The consist is "backwards", with the mail/express/baggage car at the rear, because it was not turned at Page when it arrived there as west-bound Train No. 3. The track in the foreground in the right photo is the C&O's Piney Creek branch to Lester. (Richard J. Cook photos, Lloyd D. Lewis collection)

USA class 2-8-8-2 No. 718 with a train of empties leaves the west end of Surveyor Siding minutes after meeting No. 4. This train, which originated in Elmore, will continue its work of delivering empty coal cars to the various mines along the line. (Richard J. Cook photo, Lloyd D. Lewis collection)

This is the original wooden tipple of the Mary Francis Coal Company No. 7 Mine on side tracks at Pax, Raleigh County, in June 1954. This tipple structure served its owners well but has been demolished now for several years. (C&O Railway photo, C&O Historical Society collection, CSPR 10057.E01)

A VGN EA Class 4-4-0 pulls two baggage cars, two wooden coaches and one of the road's four named wooden parlor cars through the snowy West Virginia countryside. This could be Train No. 14 approaching the Lively station eastbound. This photo was taken before World War II for sure. (Robert Keller photo, West Virginia State Archives)

From the rear platform of westbound No. 3 in June 1940, the photographer focused on Class USA 2-8-8-2 No. 704, which was, according to the lensman, "hauling something other than coal. Probably crushed rock." And quite possibly this was limestone ballast for VGN's very heavy duty right-of-way. Location appears to be Oak Hill Junction 70 years ago. The White Oak Branch off to the left out of camera range. (Stephen P. Davidson photo, Lloyd D. Lewis collection)

Pacific type (4-6-2) No. 211 has three-car Virginian mainline train No. 4 in tow at Hamilton, just east of Page, a bit late, at 9:55 am, on June 12, 1950. It consists of a combination car, with a short Railway Post Office space plus areas for express and baggage, and two coaches. After the early 1930s, Virginian trains lacked such amenities as diners, lounges, and sleeping cars. No. 4 originated at Charleston (via trackage rights over the New York Central to Deepwater as NYC No. 104), at 7:55 a.m., reached Roanoke at 4:35 p.m., where its equipment then turned around the next morning as No. 3/103 leaving Roanoke at 7:30 a.m. and arriving Charleston at 4:25 p.m. If one wanted to take the Virginian on to Norfolk an all-night layover was needed in Roanoke. Most folks transferred to N&W for the balance of that trip if desired. (Richard J. Cook Photo, TLC collection)

Westbound Extra 713 with only two hoppers and a caboose approaches Page on June 12, 1950. An odd size train for such a large locomotive – perhaps it will pick up more loads later in its run. (Richard J. Cook photo, Lloyd D. Lewis collection)

A rare photo of VGN Class AE No. 809, taken from the rear vestibule of an eastbound passenger train near Page in June 1940. It could be the pusher engine just cut off Extra 704 East in photo on the previous page, as it appears to be the same day. (Stephen P. Davidson photo, Lloyd D. Lewis collection)

Here's a fine photograph of how a front brakeman overcomes the obviously suffocating fumes, steam and smoke of a huge Virginian Railway Mallet! This condition nearly killed many a train and engine service man on Clarks Gap Mountain until VGN's famous electrification began service in 1923. This photo – copied from an apparently early 1920s issue of The National Geographic Magazine – was taken at the east end of Wriston Tunnel, about five miles east of Page, Fayette, County, on the single-track mainline. This author knows of no such photos made on Clarks Gap Mountain – but sure wishes he did. (The National Geographic Magazine, Lloyd D. Lewis collection)

A very unusual consist is shown here by a Fairbanks-Morse's photographer. Here we have approximately one-year-old Virginian Class DE-RS (which translates to "Diesel-Electric Road Switcher) No. 52 switching two or more of the railway's 10 heavy-weight passenger coaches adjacent to the Page depot. No explanation is offered with the negative but the regular pair of New River Division passenger trains – Nos. 3 and 4 operated until July 11, 1955, which was about two months after this photo was taken sometime in April 1955. Quite possibly the explanation is no more difficult than that the big No. 52 was the Page yard engine that day and the PA Class Pacific was being serviced. We don't know for sure. (Louise Harlow photo, Herbert H. Harwood collection)

West end of Page Steam Shop, which, like Elmore, did not have a turntable. August 5, 1953. (D. Wallace Johnson photo, Lloyd D. Lewis collection)

On that same day, here's the east end of Page Steam Shop. Among the locomotives visible are US Class Mallets 727, 721, 734, 730 and 710. (D. Wallace Johnson photo, Lloyd D. Lewis collection)

USA Class 2-8-8-2 Mallet No. 711 sits alongside the modern twin coaling towers, the stand-alone water column, and the sand tower at Page. August 5, 1953. (D. Wallace Johnson photo, Lloyd D. Lewis collection)

Two-year-old Class DE-RS Train Master No. 64 is shown at Page next to the now outdated steel coal dock. May 20, 1956. (H. N. Proctor photo, Lloyd D. Lewis collection)

Opposite Top: Giant Class AE 2-10-10-2 No. 803 rests between eastbound coal trains pusher runs up from Deepwater to Page and on to Oak Hill Junction and Silver Gap. At Page engine terminal. No certain date. (Lloyd D. Lewis collection)

Opposite Bottom: That may just be "Froggy" Williams with his white cap leaning out the cab window on the engineer's seatbox on August 23, 1953, as his handsome Class USB No. 722 steed rolls 73 cars of interchange time freight and lower-rated coal westbound hustling out of Page. This is probably tightly-scheduled Train No. 71 with "hot" interline freight headed for the C&O at Deepwater and the NYC at DB Tower. The goal for this time freight was to reach NYC at DB Tower by midnight every night – or VGN would have to pay the connecting road another day's demurrage fee on each car. Both the original Deepwater Railway depot and Signal Maintainer Earl May's signalman's shanty are in the left background on this bright morning. (Joseph G. Collias photo, Lloyd D. Lewis collection)

Below: You will find a no more perfect depiction of the work of the Virginian Railway than this real beauty. USB Class Mallet No. 722, on what is probably Time Freight No. 71 with 71 cars running out this day's last few miles before Deepwater and "the end of the line," is blowing hard for the Robson grade crossing on West Virginia State Route No. 61 on August 23, 1953. What makes this scene perfect is the now long-gone coal mine tipple on the hillside above. VGN predecessor Deepwater Railway's only original customer was a sawmill located behind the cameraman about one-half mile. (Joseph G. Collias photo, Lloyd D. Lewis collection)

On July 30, 1953, Class USA Mallet No. 713 as train Extra 713 East works some of its final and very productive years on a train of all-VGN empties at DB Tower, West Virginia. (D. Wallace Johnson photo, Lloyd D. Lewis collection)

The only VGN structure at West Deepwater was this tiny depot/freight station, seen here on October 27, 1936. The C&O main line passes under the nearer bridge, and the Kanawha River passes under the farther truss bridge. Beyond that bridge is DB Tower, where the VGN connected with the NYC, providing it with a second connection for westbound traffic. The VGN's original western interchange, with the C&O at Deepwater, was reached by a one-mile track from VACO Junction. (Lloyd D. Lewis collection)

This bridge from West Deepwater to DB Tower (at left) connected Virginian with the New York Central, greatly improving VGN's coal marketing scenarios – and bottom line revenues. It was opened in 1931 and was, from that day on, the official western end of the railway – at almost 435 miles from milepost A-1, located near Norfolk Terminal Station. (Virginian Railway 1946 Annual Report photo, Lloyd D. Lewis collection)

Westbound loads of West Virginia real estate and an Erie Railroad box car are led by a new Virginian Railway DE-RS 2,400-horsepower unit across Deepwater Bridge to the New York Central Railroad interchange at DB Tower in 1954. The opening of this vital span in 1931 across headwaters of the Kanawha River finally gave VGN access to vital westward markets for bituminous from its on-line mines. (Fairbanks-Morse photo by Peg Dobbin; collection of Herbert H. Harwood)

Class USA 2-8-8-2 No. 710 blasts a magnificent coal smoke plume into the Kanawha County sky. The big Mallet had been toting coal and hustling time freight for Virginian men for about 30 years when this photo was snapped on New York Central trackage rights at Cedar Grove, West Virginia, on August 23, 1953. Thousands of tons of revenue coal in 147 cars of several sizes follow the 710 this day on single track to the joint VGN-NYC terminal named Dickinson Yard at the town of Quincy just about 10 miles west of here. (Another spectacular Joseph G. Collias photo, Lloyd D. Lewis collection)

Although the Virginian only came within 30 miles of Charleston, West Virginia's capital, it reached there via trackage rights over New York Central from DB Tower, and its passenger trains served the city. Here No. 103-3, behind Pacific No. 211, has just arrived at the NYC-B&O-VGN Union Station. Mail and express are being unloaded in this busy scene while an NYC passenger train sits to the right. (Thornton Wise Photo, TLC collection)

Guyandotte Branch

Class USE 2-8-8-2 Mallet No. 742 leaves a trail of coal smoke along the Guyandotte River Valley as it pulls 39 empty hoppers to supply area coal mines on June 18, 1949, just east of Itmann. (Richard J. Cook photo, Lloyd D. Lewis collection)

The time is the late 1940s and Virginian's coal business is booming. Here is an annual report photo taken by George King Shands of the brand new, latest design high capacity mine tipple at Itmann in Wyoming County, named for coal industry pioneer Isaac T. Mann. It was four miles west of Elmore Yard, which was the site of Mann's original tipple in this area. Before this giant structure was completely leveled when the mine below it ran out of coal about 30 years ago, bituminous was loaded into mine cars and traveled as many as eight to ten miles underground before it was cleaned, sized and processed in this series of buildings. (George K. Shands photo, Lloyd D. Lewis collection)

Above: H. Reid's well known photo of USE No. 737 and its very short coal train round the bend and cross Pinnacle Creek just east of Pineville, West Virginia, on August 18, 1952. This photo ran quite large in –as he called himself – "Olden Aitch's" own hardcover VGN book. Today Norfolk Southern serves a large coal mine up a hollow to the left and behind Reid. (H. Reid photo, Lloyd D. Lewis collection)

Opposite Top: A modern Kopperston Tipple on the Guyandotte Branch. (VGN Ry photo, Lloyd D. Lewis collection)

Opposite Bottom: On its first revenue mine run, VGN's third-hand Class USE Mallet No. 737 is fresh from a complete overhaul in the erecting shop at Princeton in 1948. Down the Guyandotte River Line she rolls with a couple boxcars and loads of coal bound for either N&W or C&O at Gilbert Yard Interchange, the only station where all three Pocahontas Roads ever came together. Here is a wonderfully iconic southern West Virginia railroad scene, complete with two loaded school buses delivering Wyoming County children to school west of Baileysville on W.Va. State Route 10. Much of this area has been underwater since the mid-1970s after construction of the R. D. Bailey Dam. (George King Shands photo for a VGN annual report, Lloyd D. Lewis collection)

A close-up photo of loading coal into VGN hoppers at an unknown tipple, probably also taken by Shands as published in an early 1950s annual report to stockholders. (George K. Shands photo, Lloyd D. Lewis collection)

This Shands photo shows only part of one day's loading at a the Kopperston tipple, one of the largest and most modern on VGN. (George K. Shands photo, Lloyd D. Lewis collection)

Winding Gulf Branch

Double-headed USB No. 732 and USE No. 739 with a train of empties for Amigo and beyond are seen here at Allen Junction, two miles east of Gulf Junction in 1951. (S.K. Bolton photo, H.H. Harwood collection)

Class USA Mallet No. 708 is hauling a train along what appears to be Winding Gulf perhaps in the vicinity of Allen Junction, just above the famous, now demolished, Mullens Motor Barn. Possibly early 1950s. (Ben F. Cutler photo, Lloyd D. Lewis collection)

Brand-new Fairbanks-Morse 2,400-horsepower diesel-electric No. 54 – one of the most powerful such locomotives in early dieseldom – has stopped on the Winding Gulf Branch at Stotesbury on April 26, 1955, and her crew is getting off the unit in preparation for trading empties for loads. This is the fifth engine to be bought by VGN of its 25 "Train Masters," the largest single block of this production model – of the total of only 125 ever produced. (Fairbanks-Morse photo by Peg Dobbin – collection of Herbert H. Harwood)

First trick operator Arley U. Johnson, a long-time VGN veteran, talks on the "city phone" inside the tiny telegraph office at Amigo sometime in 1960. (Lloyd D. Lewis photo)

This scene is on the Winding Gulf Branch west of Amigo, but not where C&O is close by serving joint mines, as all hoppers are Virginian. Taken in April, 1955. (Peg Dobbin photo for Fairbanks-Morse, H.H. Harwood collection)

Perhaps one of the smallest telegraph offices on the VGN was at Amigo, where the Devils Fork branch and the Stonecoal branch left the Winding Gulf main. The telegraph office can be identified by the train order signal next to it, at the center of the photo. Sometime in 1960 (Lloyd D. Lewis photo)

This is possibly No. 50, the first of the class, shuffling cars on the Winding Gulf Branch west of Amigo, in April, 1955. Miners' homes climb the hillside beyond the tracks, perched on stilts because of the slope of the land. (Peg Dobbin photo for Fairbanks-Morse, H.H. Harwood collection)

Opposite: Possibly No. 50 once again, this time with empties at Tams, West Virginia, on the Winding Gulf Branch in April, 1950. This writer believes to be the C&O station in the middle lower center of Ms. Dobbin's photo. The largest building in this view is almost certainly the company store, and one- and two-story company houses are on the surrounding hillsides, some propped up by sturdy stilts and renting to miners and their families for perhaps $5 per month, and more for the larger ones. William P. Tams started his own coal company around 1905 and was considered a very paternalistic mine owner. He was considered so unusual that he was the subject of a long Playboy Magazine interview about 1968! Tams sold out about 1960 to the Westmoreland Coal Company, which continues mining here to this day. Perhaps we will never run out of great low-sulphur, smokeless coal in West Virginia. (Peg Dobbin photo for Fairbanks-Morse, H.H. Harwood collection)

One of the brightly painted Train Master units handles another mine shifter near the mining town of Tams in about 1958.
(Pat Dobbin photo, H.H. Harwood, Jr. collection)

Squeezed in the valley in the Winding Gulf region, Tams was the archetype of a West Virginia coal town, with its tipples, company owned houses, multiple railroad tracks, and community facilities such as the ever-present church (in the center distance). Note the Train Master locomotive with coal cars in the right foreground in this April, 1955 view. (Peg Dobbin photo, H.H Harwood, Jr. collection)

Riffes Branch Mine Tipple on VGN's Winding Gulf Branch at East Gulf, Raleigh County, seen here in June 1954. This is certainly a jointly-served mine with the C&O hoppers under the tipple. (C&O Railway photo C&O Historical Society collection, CSPR 10057.D12)

C&O loaded hoppers with Virginian empty and loaded hoppers at the C. H. Coal Company mine at Mead on VGN's Stonecoal Branch in June 1954. This is one of several jointly served coal mines on Virginian's Winding Gulf Branch. Loads were taken and empties distributed to this and the other joint mines according to the coal company's customers' instructions. Note the huge pile of slack coal laid up again the hillside for many years and what may be the company store at right. This slack coal was picked out in the cleaning process and many of these piles of waste across West Virginia burned for 50 and more years because of spontaneous combustion, creating a real pollution hazard for coal company folks. (C&O Railway photo, C&O Historical Society collection, CSPR 10057.D10)

Killarney Mine of Lillybrook Coal Company, whose metal tipple was located on Virginian's Stonecoal Branch. Taken June 1954. No coal business today and light-railed branch in foreground. (C&O Railway photo, C&O Historical Society collection, CSPR 10057.D05)

Opposite Top: Another typical mine scene is at Royal with a Train Master delivering empties to the tipple in April 1955 (Pat Dobbin photo, H.H. Harwood, Jr. collection)

Opposite Below: Train Master No. 57 has a mine shifter, probably somewhere in the Winding Gulf. Note the caboose on the far end of the locomotive. (Pat Dobbin photo, H.H. Harwood collection)

Extra 713 East lumbers downgrade through Loop Junction Tunnel on August 6, 1953. A motor car set-off track is to the left, and behind the photographer is a short bridge over the competing C&O, up from Raleigh Yard. This immediate area today is mined out and, with removal in the last few years of the ex-C&O Gulf Switchback, Norfolk Southern moves loaded CSX hoppers and delivers empties to joint mines and then moves them to nearby Pemberton for interchange. (D. Wallace Johnson photo, Lloyd D. Lewis collection)

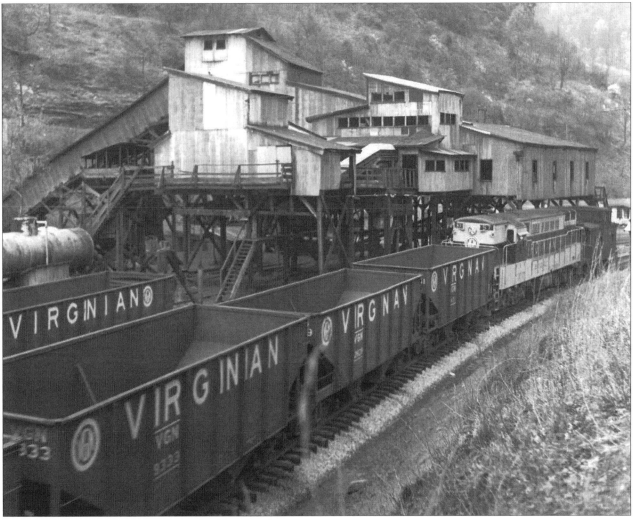

Here is one of the best known of all Virginian Railway photographs, which was most likely taken when this DE-RS unit was new. Contrary to what you might think, this picture shows both ends of the same train as it travels around the Winding Gulf Loop in the upper reaches of the Winding Gulf. O W. "Pete" Andrews, a VGN Elmore Yard Clerk, was the man who clicked the shutter on his 4x5 Speed Graphic camera after setting up this scene with the Princeton Dispatcher and probably even with the Division Superintendent there. Certainly no roads led Andrews to this point, so he climbed hillsides for at least a mile to get this treasured photo. Scene is Loop Junction Tunnel and the C&O's local mine branch up from Raleigh Yard runs under the bridge just out of the tunnel. Its right-of-way is seen just above the new unit. Surely we could do this again in 2012, with proper permission to trespass on Norfolk Southern property? (O. W. "Pete" Andrews photo, Lloyd D. Lewis collection)

Above and Below: This modern coal tipple, for the late 1940s, was served by VGN for many years. The author cannot readily identify this location – which also goes for the nice-looking coal camp dwellings for what may be the same mine. (Virginian Railway 1948 Annual Report photos probably taken by George King Shands, Lloyd D. Lewis collection)

ACKNOWLEDGEMENTS

Many thanks to all who contributed photographs to this tome. Individual photo credits are part of the captions of each of the Virginian Railway photos herein. This book – and my other three, also – would obviously be nothing without the generous support and help of my many friends. Thanks again to each of you, and let us do this again soonest.

Other fine friends who helped me immeasurably in the production of this brand new book include Thomas Ray Marshall Jr. of Mullens, W. Va., Aubrey M. Wiley of Lynchburg, Va., and, of course, my publisher and old friend from West Virginia, Tom Dixon of Lynchburg, Va.

Nota bene: No, friends, this is still not my ultimate Virginian Railway history – only my fourth! The ultimate VGN tome for this writer will be the one that Bill McClure of Richmond, Virginia, Tim Hensley of here in Kenova, and several other kind men have been urging me to write for several years.

I have lots of work and thoroughly enjoyable research to perform before my "big one" is even ready for the writing. My primary task in this regard will be to transcribe or have transcribed for me about 65 personal interviews on tape and from my own left handed penmanship. I visited these Virginian men from the fall of 1963 in my Princeton hometown, until recently, helping them recall their careers in nearly all types of railway jobs.

Other books and articles may intercede between this one and my "big one" – but this is my real goal: To have published a footnoted, annotated and very documented history of my favorite railway which I may proudly dedicate to my Dad and other VGN men whom I have known virtually all my own life.

I am just so sorry that since my third VGN book was published in 1994, because many VGN men have gone on to their great rewards in heaven since then. This one was too long in coming. But I sincerely hope all you readers enjoy my efforts. I just get such a kick out of writing anything. I've never had writer's cramp.

If any of you detect any errors of commission or omission, please address them to publisher Tom Dixon at TLC Publishing. I will appreciate this very much. I take full responsibility for any errors herein – and I sure hope they are very few and very far between. In addition, the opinions expressed are mine alone.

Also, if you have any photographs, slides, negatives, or images of any type that you would be willing to share with me, please contact Tom Dixon at TLC Publishing. He or I will promptly scan or otherwise copy them and get them back to you owners as soon as possible.

Absolutely any Virginian Railway or predecessor Deepwater or Tidewater Railway images – including but not limited to, people, locomotives, trains, freight cars, passengers cars, any and all other rolling stock, derailments of any size, etc., including any painted Norfolk & Western after merger – are really more than welcome!

And I am particularly looking for the works of the late H. Reid and the late August A. Thieme, Jr. Not only VGN but any of their photos! Thanks very much.

Lloyd D. Lewis

Kenova, West Virginia
November 1st, 2011

T.L.Wise photo, TLC collection.